ADVANCE

ADVANCE

Discover
Alignment
and
Authenticity
by
Living in
Concert
with
Your
Situation

NIC COLLINS

First edition, 2025

ISBN: 979-8-9932095-0-0 (Paperback)

ISBN: 979-8-9932095-1-7 (Hard cover)

ISBN: 979-8-9932095-2-4 (eBook)

ISBN: 979-8-9932095-3-1 (Audiobook)

Library of Congress Control Number: 2025920179

Book editing by Stanley Dankoski of The Grounded Writer

www.GroundedWriter.com

Cover design and interior formatting by Becky's Graphic Design®, LLC

www.BeckysGraphicDesign.com

Audiobook production provided by Twin Flames Studios

www.TwinFlamesStudios.com

NCA Books

For—The Fab Five

Contents

Introduction

Some way, somehow, I made my own path
I put my life on what I believe in and I do it to death
And with my last breath, I just hope that I can express
If you're looking for change, first take a look at yourself

—NiccaTine, "Look At Yourself"

AS I THINK ABOUT the lives we lead, and the many different types of situations we find ourselves in, I wonder: *How often do we deflect the opportunity to really exist in the present moment by convincing ourselves that a different situation would better suit our dream, passion, or endeavor? How often do we convince ourselves that we will get to the "life" part once we navigate the challenging situation we are currently in?*

We talk about work-life balance as if "work" and "life" are different modes of existence. We work, and if we work real hard, then we can go do "life" for a little while. No! There is no work-life balance! It's all life! It is all life in the one and only life that we have while on this Earth.

Spiritual teacher Eckhart Tolle has said something that I love and come back to time and time again: "Forget about your life situation and pay attention to your life," he said. "Your life situation exists in time. Your life is now. Your life situation is mind-stuff. Your life is real." This has taught me so much about presence, about the importance of returning to our true essence. It's taught me that somewhere—beneath the distraction-laden, manufactured, fabricated bullshit—lies this exact moment. In challenge and heartache, we are living our life right now. In joy and success, as well as in the mundane, our life is now.

Authenticity is the fulcrum, anchoring the balance of your life and your life situation, allowing them to coexist in harmony. At a minimum, they run in parallel paths. Oxford defines "authentic" as being of undisputed origin. You are one of one, undisputedly *you*. You are authentically made. With authenticity, we gain the ability to show up in any situation as our true, genuine self, and fully experience our life. Our life right now, in real time.

Some of these might resonate with you as they have with me:

I'll take that trip when. . .

I'll leave this company when. . .

I'll start having people over for dinner when. . .

I'll get back in shape when. . .

I'll finally write that book when. . .

I'll focus more on myself when. . .

When???

When are you actually going to do the thing that you are convinced will bring you joy?

When are you going to prioritize yourself? Your physical and mental health? Your well-being?

That's what this book is about. Priority. This book is about living in alignment and about becoming the most pure, authentic version of yourself, regardless of the situation or circumstance. Better yet, in spite of the situation or circumstance. This book is about rediscovery and taking a renewed interest and focus on *you*.

The journey of life can feel complicated. Familial, cultural, and environmental influences are present to guide us in certain directions. We are inundated with sales pitches, targeted marketing, and propaganda designed to steer us in the direction of products and services. Societal conditioning, wherever you may live, is a force stronger than many of us realize, pushing us toward outcomes without choosing them for ourselves.

My hope is that the words in this book act as a guiding and helpful resource—and this resource says it's time to sit in the driver's seat and grab the wheel of *your* life, the one and only life that you have on this Earth. But, before you take the wheel, it's for you to decide what type of vehicle you want to drive, if you even want a vehicle at all, or if you prefer seeing the world at a cyclist's pace. It's all up to you.

Breaking down conditioning, limiting beliefs, and habitual behaviors can be a daunting task. Self-discovery, personal growth, and exploring meaning in your life is an extremely tall order. It's not easy. But it is essential if you are in pursuit of living up to your potential. As opposed to living only to make the most money in a role, to satisfy the people around you, or to look as if you have it all figured out. Living up to *your* potential is the potential to be the best, most aligned, and content version of yourself.

This type of work gets difficult, messy, and scary. This book welcomes the difficult, messy, and scary parts. It highlights them, dissects them, and creates a space for you to walk your own path. Change is hard. Growth is hard. Being honest with yourself and accepting that a former belief, which you swore up and down was the *truth* and now no longer feels accurate, is hard. Being open to the possibility that the idea of who you will be and what you'll be doing in six months, one year, ten years, maybe hasn't even been conceived yet, is hard. The unknown is incredibly hard. But is it worth it?

What is the cost of *not* growing? The cost of *not* ever finding out what fuels your soul? The limits you are capable of blowing past? I have never heard of anyone in their final days applauding their life decisions that kept them stagnant, comfortable, and just like everyone else.

This is about celebrating who you already are, and growing into a new and improved iteration of yourself.

I often hear the idea that we must kill off former versions of ourselves, or mourn the loss of the person we once were. Those former versions, warts and all, are all a part of who we are up until the very last breath. The former versions teach and inform us, and our future versions can inspire and guide us, and offer hope in darkness. I look at this in the way that a snake sheds its skin. I am still the same animal, but I have outgrown old behaviors, friends, jobs, beliefs, challenges, situations, and approaches. We are fortunate to have the ability to shed all that no longer serves us, and to come out a renewed, regenerated, bigger, and badder MF'er than ever before!

My hope is that in this book I have created a space for you to explore every part of yourself, with openness, curiosity, and vulnerability. I mean *all* of the parts, not just the parts already out in the open, in full exposure to everyone, but also the parts in the back corner of your dark, dusty garage closet, with old dried up paint cans and rusty tools sitting on some spilled oil. No judgment, no comparison.

I have lived my own wild journey that brought me right here to this very place with you. My journey is mine, yours is yours. It is not my hope that you proceed in a way that is consistent with my life, but that my sharing vulnerably may be helpful in your pursuit of discovering your most authentic self, and in living in concert with *your* situation.

Working through mental health challenges and substance use in my teens and twenties led to a lifelong bout of self-discovery and personal growth. In no way am I "fixed," nor do I have all of the answers, but I have dedicated my life to becoming a person whom I can look at in the mirror each day and be proud of. There are good days, bad days, and sometimes just plain ol' days. I am not where I know that I can be yet, but I sure as hell am not where I used to be either, and that feels satisfying. I want that for you, to be able to look in the mirror and know the person looking back, accept, and be proud of them. And I hope that you want that for yourself.

After nearly two decades in corporate America working in industrial sales, I pivoted to pursue a graduate degree in mental health counseling and rehabilitation. I find meaning in life by serving others, and working in counseling felt like a place that aligned with my values and spoke directly to my skillset. I know that, in order to use my skills, education, lived experiences, and expertise to help others, it is imperative that I first take care of myself. This is true for all of us.

As I drove a van across America for a couple of months in the summer of 2024, I reflected on all of the lessons I learned throughout the course of my life thus far. These realizations have come from my own lived experience as well as the experiences of others. They have come from research, reading, and learning; observing, witnessing, and watching. These experiences, lessons, and realizations are layered throughout this book. What I share here is a culmination of theories, philosophies, and implementations that I have realized to be integral to living in truth, fulfillment, and alignment.

The first part of the book shares implementations that you can deploy right away, a guide to help you find empowerment in prioritizing *you* and taking back control of your own life, perhaps for the first time. The second part of the book houses nonlinear, inexact, imperfect steps that have led me to understand what it means to live in full authenticity.

These pages express how I have learned to prioritize and care for myself so that I am able to best serve others. How I have become open to change, acknowledge my emotions, and to step outside of my comfort zone. To practice gratitude and be present. To be intentional with my time, and engage in my life in a way that lights my freaking soul on fire. I invite you to do the same, and I am so happy that you are here.

Let's ADVANCE together.

PART I

IMPLEMENT

REALIZATION

Engage

Having purpose and belonging

The difference between engaging and not can be like the difference between "in sickness and in health." In fact, not *like* that—it *can* be that. Here's a story of one person who experienced these polar opposites and how engagement changed her life for the better.

When I was getting my master's degree in mental health counseling, I sat in a class on psychiatric rehabilitation. We were discussing self-determination theory, which explores human psychology, personality, and growth, and the motivation behind them. It suggests that a person directs their behavior based on their desires and needs, personally and socially. The idea is that we as humans are most motivated through autonomy, competence, and relatedness.

We were examining a case study of an individual, whom I'll call Genevieve, who was diagnosed with schizophrenia and struggling to find employment. Genevieve's doctors believed she was unable to hold quality, sustainable employment due to her symptoms of schizophrenia. She had hallucinations and would often hear voices in her head. As difficult as it may have been to live with these symptoms daily, being faced with this feedback from her doctor began a chain reaction into other areas of her life. She became depressed, the hallucinations became more severe, and she had more and more trouble completing tasks like laundry, cooking, and hygiene.

Her schizophrenia aside, consider the ripple that occurs in our own lives when we feel outcast, isolated, overlooked, or lonely. Those feelings have a tendency to dictate our mood, then spill over into our personal and social relationships, which likely drags down our ability to function appropriately at work. The feelings and their effects are all connected, overwhelming us until we feel life snowballing, gaining momentum down the side of a mountain. When we're overlooked, it feels as though we are insignificant. When we're outcast, it may invoke extreme anger, possibly even conflict. Loneliness and isolation leave us in seemingly inescapable bouts of sadness, and can lead to severe depression. The snowball grows in size and picks up speed.

We often ask our psychiatrist or therapist, "Am I crazy? Do I have X, Y, or Z disorder?" If the answer is no, we think: *Whew! Nothing is wrong with me!* But then we jump back in that oversized, habitual snowball, unaware that it's becoming an avalanche. We jump back in, often without reflecting or paying any attention to how we may have gotten to this point.

The reality is that we all land somewhere on the spectrum of symptoms for many of these disorders, diagnosable or not. Of course, it's difficult for us to admit that we feel depressed or lonely, so we button up those feelings and keep on keeping on. "Button up" does not even do it justice. It is probably more like shoving these feelings as deep into the abyss as we can, then stitching them up, applying duct tape, burying them in the ground, and pouring concrete on top.

Back to Genevieve: Although her symptoms seemed to be worsening, she felt like she continued to get the same feedback from professionals justifying why things had gotten so difficult for her. They would walk her through case studies of schizophrenia and describe how the symptoms prohibit her from living a "normal" life like that of her family and friends. She was told how to best manage her symptoms in order to maximize her situation based on the diagnosis. That is, until she began working with a psychiatrist named Doctor Mulwig.

She began seeing Dr. Mulwig weekly. She was able to express how she used to feel, and how she desperately missed that sense of belonging. She explained how her symptoms had gotten so bad that she could not hold a job, and as a result her mental health had spiraled. Dr. Mulwig, after several weeks of getting to understand and know Genevieve better, felt like it was time to help her in search of a vocation. Of course, Genevieve was nervous to take on this task, given her recent history and disappointment. But she would be monitored by Dr. Mulwig periodically and continue to see him for her regular weekly sessions. He assured her that together they would assess the situation to determine a path forward, so she agreed to give it a shot.

He helped her land a job in the cafeteria of a military facility. She was to greet the soldiers as they came in to eat lunch and to replenish the trays of food items on the cafeteria line, all while serving them their meals. She was one of five employees working different roles within the cafeteria. To start out, she was on base for five hours per shift, five days per week. The role had the eventual opportunity to work the evening meal, which would get her up to eight hours per day, forty hours per week. This was a lofty goal, considering she had been having trouble completing her normal daily tasks, but Dr. Mulwig was adamant that she remain open.

After a couple of weeks, Doctor Mulwig visited Genevieve on the job. He sat in the corner of the cafeteria at first simply observing the process, and how she was responding. After about fifteen minutes of watching, he decided to go up and ask her how she felt it had been going. Several times he tried to get a quick word with her. She blew him off, saying, "Can't talk, too busy!" The psychiatrist was encouraged and slightly surprised by witnessing her ability to engage with each soldier as they passed through her line *and* quickly serve their meal.

Eventually she had a short break, and they were able to talk.

"So, how are you able to manage the hallucinations and voices?" the psychiatrist asked.

"I don't have time for them right now," Genevieve replied.

It's amazing what can happen when we engage. We feel a sense of purpose and belonging. Genevieve was so busy fulfilling her work obligations that she had not thought about her schizophrenia at all, and her symptoms seemingly disappeared. Better yet, no one there that day noticed anything out of the ordinary with the way she was interacting.

Are we sitting around trying to prevent every little thing that "might" happen to us, yet are still feeling anxious, depressed, and unhappy? Or are we helping a friend build a fence, hiking a mountain, calling a relative, going to a play, or trying something new? At work, are we constantly thinking of the things that suck about this place, or are we grateful for the opportunity to make an impact, learn something new, or build relationships?

Taking the first step

Engagement has nothing to do with completion, and it has absolutely nothing to do with perfection. Engagement has everything to do with a willingness to start, and ultimately, connection. We can engage in the stillness of a meditative practice or the all-out effort of an ultramarathon, and the value is only fully recognized through connection: connecting with self, with others, and with nature.

Self-discovery provides the foundation for contentment and is a prerequisite to having sustained, successful relationships with others. Truly connecting with people offers flavor and color to our life, and is an essential component of the human condition. Nature offers presence and peace, and an awareness of a bigger picture of which we are an integral part.

It is so easy to tell ourselves that we are not ready yet, that we don't have a clear enough vision. We can talk ourselves out of anything. If we don't know exactly what the finish line looks like, or the perfect route to get there, we bow out. To make it worse, we convince ourselves we made a wise, mature decision because we mitigated risk and did not act impulsively or rashly. What really has happened in most cases, is that fear and doubt have taken over before the vehicle ever got in motion.

I was recently at an event and had the opportunity to hear singer Mike Posner speak and perform some of his songs. Mike rose to a level of notoriety while attending Duke University when he released his song "Cooler Than Me." He traveled the world performing, and was eventually nominated for a Grammy. In recent years, his traveling the world led him to walking across the United States of America, from New Jersey to California, and later standing atop the tallest mountain on the planet.

He talked to us that evening in a field in north Georgia about his journey across America. He shared his five steps to happiness and how they were organically developed as he put one foot in front of the other for six months walking across a continent. It all started with a crazy idea to complete this adventure. His first lesson was one of my favorite lines, and I use it often as a gauge for my own ideas: "Not all crazy ideas are great, but all great ideas are crazy."

So he had this idea, and sure, he had to plan logistically and financially to turn this idea into a reality. But what he had to do next is what I believe is the hardest part for many of us. We find ourselves in analysis paralysis, making sure everything is perfect, and ready, and just right. That does not move the needle. So, his second gem of wisdom in the pursuit of happiness is that *step one is to take one step.* I got chills when I heard Mike Posner say this in person, because even people who have sold millions of records, walked across America, and climbed Mount Everest have to start somewhere. We have to start. Starting—engaging—is what creates connection, and connection leads to meaning and fulfillment.

Worry and doubt fill our minds and we can become fearful of making a wrong step, so we defer to stagnation. Y'all, first we just have to walk. That's it. When we start, let's say we accidentally went in an unfavorable direction. Going down that path could show us exactly what we need to get going in the perceived "right" direction! We don't need to know exactly where the finish line is, we don't have to walk on a tightrope in a linear and perfect direction. We don't have to walk as far as the next person. We just have to walk. Take one step. Take another step. You can climb mountains, figuratively and literally.

Following the DGP model

It's easy to get caught up in the whirlwind that comes with routine, goal setting, and process-driven behavior. A common feeling of overwhelm, expectation, and pressure whips up when attempting to assemble the perfect routine, set goals, and build processes. They've become buzz words, and there are more than enough ads telling us what we "should" be doing. We know they're important, but it can be exhausting. Each holds incredible value, but the recipe is incomplete without engagement.

Consider that goals are valuable, but prior to setting goals, reflection and value identification are also important. So, if we are setting goals in an area that does not fulfill a purpose or passion, was it helpful to set the goal? SMART goals are wonderful, and I believe in them, but it is not necessarily useful to work towards something specific, measurable, attainable, relevant, and timely that does not serve the larger vision.

I created a model to help me understand this construct whenever I feel lost in decision making. It's called the DGP model. It simply stands for Dream/Goal/Process. We often talk about goal-driven behavior—choosing something to shoot for and working directly to achieve that thing—and trusting the process. Both are vital to our growth. To those concepts, I simply add starting with a Dream.

We tell our children to dream when they are young. Your parents likely told you that you could be anything you wanted to be when you grow up. Do you still believe that? Why do we stop dreaming?

Before we set goals and focus on a process, it is helpful to identify what you actually care about in life. What moves you? What do you think about when you lie awake in bed at night? What are your values? What do you consider purposeful? The answers to these questions might provide a general area of focus, a direction in which to move to create momentum. Within that area of focus, we may then identify goals that support our overall vision.

Goals can shift over time, but it's likely we won't have to make an about face because we started with dreaming, with our imagination. This movement was led by our intuition and our soul. As we set targets, or goals, it helps us to zoom in on what we believe we want to accomplish, on our dream.

Process, then, becomes the vehicle that moves us in the direction of those targets. In fact, it's the vessel in which we choose to move through life. It shows up as our morning routines and daily habits. It's who we surround ourselves with, the environments we put ourselves in, the food we use to fuel our bodies. One of my favorite quotes is: "How we spend our days is how we spend our lives." That speaks directly to our process.

So, first, dream. Understand what you care about and what moves you. Then, set targets within that vision as a point of reference. Finally, build habits and take actions today that move you in that direction. Set the goal, then detach from the fixation of the goal itself. This provides us with a structure and the flexibility to do what best serves us in the present moment.

Take action today. That's the glue that holds this model together. It is more than glue; it's fuel that creates momentum and propels us forward. That is engagement. We are building our ship as it sails. We are all figuring it out, whatever "it" is. We experience life differently once we engage. It infuses our experiences with color and life. When we sit around and wait for things to change, it is likely they never will. And if they do, it is more likely that we are not satisfied with that change. Are you a bystander in your own life?

Meet yourself where you are

When working through the DGP model, it is important to be honest. Meet yourself and assess where you're at, acknowledge any perceived limitations, and take action. Imperfect action trumps inaction. We each have our own obstacles and challenges impeding the next step, but it is most certainly doable.

Earlier in my life, I was going through a period where I was struggling with severe depression. As many of you may know, depression has a tendency to take over. It will kick you right out of the driver's seat of your own life, refuse to wear a seat belt, and put the pedal to the medal. At the time, I was not happy with the state of my life so I stayed inside my house more. I was tired of seeing and hearing how happy others were, so I spent more time alone. The time I spent alone was not rich in self exploration or even contentment, but more in disgust and anger.

To combat those feelings, I drank excessively. As I drank more, I had less money because I was spending it all either on, or because of, alcohol. I was hungover most of the time, so my performance at work continuously slipped. Work took so much out of me that I did not ever feel like keeping in touch with my family on evenings and weekends. By then, I felt so worthless, to the point where I believed I was such a disappointment to them. I convinced myself they were better off without hearing from me. I was sure the world was better off without me.

Sadly, this is an extremely common story in our society. We've either experienced, or known someone who has experienced, some version of this story. Many are living it right now, and they feel helpless, isolated, and alone. It's not my intention here to tell anyone what they should do, but simply to share my experience and some things that I have found to be helpful, with the hope it could possibly be valuable to someone else.

First, I would like to speak to those that know someone in a similar situation to what I described above. It is incredibly encouraging how many people there are who care and are willing to help. Without them, the outlook on our collective mental health would be much more bleak.

Let's dig deeper on what it means to help. Help does not equal advice.

Help does not equal fixing. In fact, help might not even be the appropriate word to use. To help someone implies doing. Oftentimes, when we do not know exactly how to handle a difficult situation, we resort to making ourselves busy. By *doing* something. There is plenty of discussion in this book about action, and it is integral to progress. There is also an undervalued importance in *being*.

When someone you care about is in the midst of something difficult for them—a breakup, depression, grief, worthlessness—they are almost never asking you what they *should* do next. Whatever brilliant, obvious advice you have for them, I can assure you they have already thought of it. This is not a time for you to show off your solution-focused philosophy or your knowledge of Lean or Six Sigma–type efficiencies.

If you truly want to help, you must realize this is not about you at all. This is an opportunity to just be. And listen. If their logic doesn't make any sense, listen. If their conversation goes in circles, listen. If they voice regret over doing something that you suggested over a million times they avoid, maybe flash a subtle, acknowledging (and internally slightly satisfying) grin, nod your head, and then, *listen*. Please do not ever opt out of being there for someone in fear of not having the right words. Your presence is all that is required.

Now, immediately after saying "advice is not what someone needs when they are in crisis," I am going to tip-toe that line and aim to offer something in hopes it could be useful. When in crisis with severe depression or thoughts of suicide, getting through the moment is the only objective. It is all that matters. Whatever is needed to bridge the gap to the next living, breathing moment, do it, by any means necessary. We need you here in this world.

There were nights where I did not think I would be around to see the light of another day. I would then get hammered drunk, smoke weed, and listen to the most depressing and vengeful music I could access until I passed out. Then, I woke up the next day. Those are not the habits I necessarily endorse or engage in today, but they did play a significant role in getting me here. I have not taken a sip of alcohol since April 13, 2019, a very proud accomplishment. That said, if I were back in one of those times where I didn't think I could get through the night, I would do it all over again in a heartbeat.

Those ways of coping were vital. That is what bridged the gap for me, on more occasions than I can count. It was the thinnest, most frayed thread ever, and I held onto it while weeping and gasping for air. But I held on. Whatever that thread is to keep you connected to this life, hang on to it with everything you've got. I am forever grateful for that connection.

Remember when I said engagement has everything to do with connection? That is why this is the first realization in this book. Long before I ever realized it, engagement kept me alive. It feels slightly twisted to say that, because it feels like it's not what is "supposed" to be talked about. Which means I absolutely should talk about it, because for me, and maybe for you, it is the truth.

This speaks to something bigger than us. Those connections are what led to the development of the DGP model, which I introduced in the previous chapter. Dreaming allowed me eventually to explore purpose, connection, and belonging in a more healthy and positive way. Dreaming sometimes begins while we engage in unhealthy options, what we call bad habits. I'm not suggesting taking imperfect action so you can justify behaviors and actions that you know are not serving your overall well-being. I certainly encourage engaging in positive behaviors, *and* I acknowledge that growth and progress often start before we realize. It is not always a pretty, perfectly packaged manual that we can sell to others to show the way. It is often ugly, messy, nonlinear, at times dangerous, and scary.

Somewhere in the landslide that I had found myself in, I sat on a couch in what I viewed as my own version of *Good Will Hunting*. I agreed to see a therapist in a last-ditch effort to hold on to a failing relationship. No other reason than that—or so I thought. Whatever the driving force was that landed me on the couch that day, it changed the trajectory of my life forever. A conversation that began with my anger and bitterness over a girl evolved into a decade-long bout of self-exploration, awareness, discovery, and growth. I don't have the benefit of comparison to say where I would be today, if even here at all, had I not engaged in therapy. But I do know that my willingness to show up every Tuesday at 11:00 and dig in, allowed me to connect with myself in a way I didn't previously know was possible.

I realized that disengaging from relationships with family, friends, and my interests had been contributing greatly to my depression and downward spiral, which likely began in college nearly a decade prior. I had been searching and yearning for some monumental, defining, magical moment to land in my lap *before* I felt equipped and significant enough to interact. When in fact, merely interacting with people and things that once mattered to me enabled me to feel a sense of worth.

We all know that comparison is the thief of joy, so it does not matter where someone else is on the scale of engagement. What matters is that we do something we haven't previously done. It makes me think of the definition of insanity, about doing the same things and expecting different results.

Some areas of engagement that helped create some momentum for me early on were running a 5K, calling my family, and picking up a musical instrument. All of those came with a level of discomfort at the time, and that is OK. Take a sizable enough bite that might make your jaw sore from chewing, but not enough to choke you. Even if it makes you cough a little bit, you will be better equipped for the next ambitious bite.

What is something you can challenge yourself to begin working toward today?

Trying something new

We never know what could come our way by simply trying something new. We do know, however, what the result will be if we never try. Signing up for a 5K and running it was a success. I did something I had not done in quite a while, and it got my competitive juices flowing. My performance didn't land me on the podium, and that wasn't my measure of success, but I did get out of my comfort zone. I pushed myself and was pleased with the accomplishment. If that were the end of the story, it would be a win.

However, that is not the end of the story. It felt so good to get outside and exert some energy, that it kickstarted what is currently a streak of more than six years of completing at least a 5K worth of steps every single day. I have done 5Ks in one-hundred degree heat and in driving snow. I have done 5Ks at sea level and at over fourteen thousand feet of elevation. I have done 5Ks in airports, other countries, cities, deserts, rainforests. I have done them alone, and I have done them with thousands of people.

The idea of running every day, for what was initially a one-month challenge for myself, planted the seed for an idea that I expanded well beyond running. I will share more on that later, but that never would have been developed or put into practice had I not run the first 5K.

My entire perspective on running changed via running a 5K every day for a month. Where it used to feel like work or punishment for eating like shit, it soon began to feel like a privilege I was fortunate to have the opportunity to engage in. I became so grateful for running.

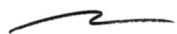

I remember that the first time I signed up for a 50K, I didn't really know what a 50K was. I mean, 13.1 miles was the farthest distance I had ever run at the time, and a 50K is 31 miles. I guess I thought it would be cool to flip the numbers from one-three to three-one. I had no business making this jump. But something gave me the idea, and I floated it by my friend Jordan. I knew him to be a "runner," so I figured he had the appropriate wisdom and logic to impart if this were too terrible of an idea.

Jordan had worked for a local running store, timed races, and sold me all of my running shoes. The few times I did see him actually run, it was only for a few seconds at the beginning of a race when he took off like he was shot out of a cannon, leaving me comfortably in his wake. What I did not know back then was that, the more of a runner someone was, the less likely logic was to make an appearance. The best I remember, there was dangerously little discussion around the idea, and almost immediately we were booking a hotel.

It's worth noting this wasn't just a regular ol' 50K either. This was a backyard ultra from the creative and distorted mind of Matt Hammersmith. It was called The Longest Day. It dons that title because it was, in fact, on the longest day of the year, June 20, 2020. A backyard ultra is unique in its design because it allows for the race to be held over a small geography. These are loop-style races where you run multiple laps of a much shorter course to reach your full distance. This particular race was on a 1.9-mile course, mostly through the woods, that we were to run sixteen times to complete the thirty-one-mile ultramarathon. Another zinger was that you could only begin a lap at a specific time. The first lap started at 6:30am. The second lap began 45 minutes later. Third lap, 44 minutes after that. Fourth lap, 43 minutes; fifth, 42, and so on. You could take as long as you wanted on a lap, as long as you were back to the start line in time for the next lap. So by design, we were out there ALL DAY LONG with less and less time in between laps. And, oh yeah, this race was in South Carolina, where the sun, heat, and humidity are not typically known to hold anything back.

When I say my friend Jordan was a runner, I mean both that he had been consistently running for many years *and* that he is fast. By my standards, real fast. He unofficially became my coach. Though he had competed at a high level, and run many races, he had only run two full marathons ever. His first was just for shits and gigs to see if he could qualify for the Boston marathon. And his second, the Boston marathon. They don't just let anybody in that race, from what I understand. But he had never run an ultramarathon, and he wasn't much of a trail runner. The closer we got to the event, the more I realized this was not something he was entirely comfortable with either. I guess we were both stepping outside of our comfort zones to challenge ourselves, and we had each other to blame for this ridiculous, questionable idea.

We had a tailgate tent set up adjacent to the start/finish line that housed a couple of tailgate chairs, an incredible spread of salty and sugary snacks, and a change of shoes. That was our home base for the day, a place we could take a quick breather in between laps and check in with (or lie to) each other about our physical and mental well-being. It was our first rodeo in this setting, so we initially kept to ourselves. For everyone else, it just appeared to be a social event. People were laughing and hugging, a few even drinking cold beer between laps.

During one of our breaks in between laps, probably around halfway, we overheard some of our tent neighbors talking. We did not hear the full context, but one of the ladies said, "Yeah, we saw them at the last ultra we ran. They had never run further than a half marathon, and somehow they thought they were going to be able to run thirty-one miles!" Everyone within earshot died laughing. Well, everyone except me. Even Jordan got in a nice chuckle. I started to panic. What did they know about what was about to happen to me that I didn't know? What *was* about to happen to me? Why did I decide to do something I clearly had no business doing? Why did Jordan agree to a front row seat to my inevitable demise? Because he thought it would be funny to see me crash and burn?

These thoughts were running rampant in my mind, all while the seconds were ticking down to the start of our next lap. I felt a lump in my throat. I considered not continuing the event, justifying it as a wise move to prevent whatever these people knew that I didn't from happening. How mature of me.

Jordan would not let that happen. He told me I was not going to let that happen. He asked how I felt, and surprisingly, other than general fatigue and soreness, I felt pretty good. He told me all I had to do was get to the start line. I had allowed all of this doubt from a bunch of strangers to infiltrate my entire mindset. They didn't know me. Perhaps I didn't know me.

I made it back to the start line for that lap at the midway point. And the next lap, and the next lap, seven more times until I stood at the start line of my sixteenth lap. Filthy, smelly, beaten, and broken, I stood there taking it all in. We have no idea what we are capable of. I had no idea if I could run thirty-one miles that day, but maybe I could run 1.9 miles sixteen times. The bottom dropped out, the gun sounded, and we were off.

Jordan had always teased me because I would say that I was not a runner. It just didn't feel right to say it. He, and most people I had met through the running community, were much faster than me. I hadn't been doing it for long, and I just didn't feel like I had earned that identity yet. As my 5K time grew faster and faster, he would always meet me at the finish line and ask, "you a runner yet?" And each time I blew him off with a dismissive "nahhh." I could never really be a runner, because I was depressed, overweight, good-for-nothing, never-gonna-be-fast-enough, blah blah blah.

But on that June day in the South Carolina heat, my perspective and that repetitive narrative, the one I had been telling myself for so many years, changed. I had engaged. I had just run thirty-one miles, more than doubling the longest distance I had ever run. I left it all out there on the course, unable to control the tears of accomplishment and joy as I crossed the finish line.

After the race, we shuffled slowly and awkwardly into a local restaurant there in Travelers Rest, South Carolina. The bartender came over to take our order. "Hey man," Jordan said to me, "how about you tell the bartender what you did today." Proudly, and without hesitation, I said "I am an ultramarathon runner." Don't tell Jordan, but I have been a runner ever since.

In just a few years, after wondering whether or not I was in decent enough shape to sign up for a local 5K, I have run two full marathons, seven ultramarathons, and a dozen Spartan Beasts. It becomes a habit to continue expanding your comfort zone. It still takes intentionality and effort, but that muscle starts to build. Not the muscle that gives us the answers before we jump into something, but the muscle that enables us to continue jumping into the somethings we might not be totally prepared for, because the possibilities are endless.

Spend Intentional Time Alone

Prioritize Time Alone

Time spent alone is not created equally.

Time spent alone also often involves more than one person.

These statements might seem contradictory at first, but I will explain further as we move along.

It is common for people to exclaim "I need some 'me' time!" or "I'm taking a mental health day." I couldn't agree more that it is important to spend time on mental health. We owe this to ourselves, and it is up to us to be proactive in caring for our mental well-being. We get an annual physical, we go to the doctor when we don't feel well, we get a teeth cleaning twice a year, and we visit with our financial advisor. Why wouldn't we also invest our time and energy in our mental health? And when we do find some of that rare, precious time to ourselves, how are we spending it? Spending intentional time alone does not mean watching episodes three through nine of season six of *Shameless*. That is not to say don't watch *Shameless*. It's just not what we are talking about right here.

Time spent alone is not created equally, mostly because how we spend that time is up to us. Do we think, listen, feel, reflect, relax, exercise, rest, meditate, cry? Or do we avoid, scroll, ignore, deflect, play video games, binge watch Netflix, over-eat? Feel free to manipulate this list to reflect what truly feels useful to you. The first list may not be *all* right, and the second list may not be *all* wrong, but they are certainly different. The words in the first grouping take awareness and intention. Most of them are simple, but not always easy. It not only takes intention to engage with yourself in this way by looking inward, it also takes serious intention to carve out the time to make it possible. It is a common societal norm to overload our schedule, grind our bodies and minds into the ground, and care for ourselves last. Is it that we feel guilty serving ourselves when others are in need? Do we lose sight of what we truly value and dispropor-tionately allocate time to what we feel has become what we are "supposed to" do? Or are we afraid of what we might actually find by pulling back the curtain of this complex, unique, and capable soul that is me?

When I think about spending time on what is truly important, I recall Jim Valvano's speech at the ESPYs in 1993. Valvano, more commonly known as Jimmy V, had previously been the head men's basketball coach at NC State University. In 1983 he led the Pack, as a six seed, on an improbable, underdog journey through March Madness. The run began with a double overtime victory over a lower seeded Pepperdine. That was immediately followed by a one-point win over third seed UNLV. They reeled off three more victories against Utah, Virginia, and Georgia and found themselves facing off against heavily favored, top seed Houston in the championship game. In the end of a low-scoring thriller, NC State were anointed as national champions.

Ten years after cutting down the nets in what was the pinnacle of his coaching career, Jimmy V stood on the stage at the ESPY awards ceremony as the recipient of the inaugural Arthur Ashe Courage and Humanitarian Award. He had been diagnosed with cancer a year earlier, and by this point it had metastasized to his bones. His fight with cancer was one of courage and hope, and he bravely addressed the crowd that night at Madison Square Garden in what would be his last public appearance. He died less than two months later.

This is an excerpt from his ESPY speech:

> *To me, there are three things we all should do every day. . . .*
> *Number one is laugh. You should laugh every day. Number*
> *two is think. You should spend some time in thought. And*
> *number three is you should have your emotions move to tears.*
> *Could be happiness or joy, but think about it. If you laugh,*
> *you think, and you cry, that's a full day. That's a heck of a*
> *day. You do that seven days a week, you're going to have*
> *something special.*

To be honest, I get emotional every time I hear it. My emotions just moved me to tears simply writing this. It makes me think about how we tend to overcomplicate things. How we fill our lives with so many things. So many efficiencies, routines, strategies, and metrics. All of those are important, but to me they should never be done at the expense of the things Jimmy V was talking about. This was a man who knew he was dying of cancer, and this is how he measured the value of his days. What a rich experience of a life if we are able to do those things: laugh, think, and cry. Why do we consistently put ourselves last when, at the end, we are all we have?

Are you intentional with your time alone? Do you view time spent reflecting, thinking, and feeling as valuable? Are you open to carving out time for yourself to really look within?

Warren Buffett, and founders Sara Blakely, Richard Branson, and Bill Gates have all spoken about the importance of scheduling time to think. Probably the most publicized example of this is Bill Gates spending a couple of weeks each year reading and thinking. This is what he felt the most beneficial thing to do during his tenure at Microsoft. Not in retirement, not sometime down the road, but right now. Warren Buffett said, "I insist on time being spent, almost every day, to just sit and think." He *insists!* Not just gets happy when it randomly happens, but it's of the highest priority within his daily routine to do nothing but spend time alone in thought.

Richard Branson says: "When it comes to innovating, you have to give yourself the time and space to think big, to look at the stars, to chase moonshots." Not to fill your calendar with as many things as you can, but to prioritize time to yourself so that you can explore what is within you. Only once we realize what we have to share, can we truly and fully share it with the world.

While Sara Blakely was building her self-starter, home-grown empire of Spanx, she consistently scheduled time to think. She did her best thinking while she was driving. Only living a few miles from headquarters in Atlanta, she actually built in a longer commute to work just so she could think each day! Eventually she set up cameras in her vehicle so that she could capture ideas, thoughts, and reflections that came from this intentional time alone.

Doing this benefits all, not just you

It might be helpful to understand that solo time does, almost always, involve more than one person. What do I mean by that, and how could that be, since the mere definition of being "alone" would restrict the addition of any other people? That's true, but others are certainly impacted, both in the present moment when you are by yourself, and in future moments others share with you. Fairly easily, we assess time spent alone as selfish, and perhaps even that we are being unfair to those important to us. That is simply not the case. In fact, spending intentional time alone could be one of the more selfless acts in which we engage.

Having time when you can remove yourself from interacting with others is a position of privilege, and that should not be taken lightly. Acknowledging the sacrifices and support of others to make your alone time possible can help with how that time is valued. You can have the perspective that you are inconveniencing others, and you can experience guilt and negative self-talk. Or, you could take the perspective that, because of the support and encouragement of others, you have the incredible opportunity to grow into a refined evolution of yourself. Everyone wins. You have the power to shift your perspective from a self-deprecating negative attitude to one of gratitude.

It is possible that scheduling and pursuing your time alone may be a strain on a partnership, and it may lead to difficult conversations. That is OK. Of course, each situation stands on its own merit, and I'm not suggesting a one-size-fits-all, because it looks different for everyone. I am suggesting, however, to lean into those difficult conversations. It will take grace and understanding on both sides if this is a new pursuit for you. We are humans—we are scared of new and different—but we should also be excited for what lies on the other side of some discomfort and intentional engagement.

There are many possible approaches to spending this intentional time alone, so what I am about to speak about is what works for me. What works for you might be incrementally working toward something similar, or it might be ripping the band-aid off and jumping in head first. I am excited to hear what will have worked for you.

Before I get into my structure, I'll remind you that this really is time alone. It will be difficult. Set the phone down, or leave it in the vehicle. Check in less. Lean into the boredom. Let emotions flow. Be open. You can share all of your experiences with your significant other upon your return, but in the moment it is about *your* thoughts, feelings, and experience. We will not reach our best connection with a partner without first connecting with and understanding ourselves.

Identifying our solo missions

Each year, typically the second week of January, I spend several days in solitude in the mountains of north Georgia. For the past five years I have made this a priority in my life, to the point I would call it a nonnegotiable. It is a time when I am able to unplug from electronics and plug into the natural world around me. It is a time when I pour into myself, through meditation, reflection, and planning. I mostly spend time outside in nature, while also turning inside to my body, my feelings, and my emotions. Simply writing about it here makes me ready to go back.

It is important to identify the things we feel hold this type of importance in our lives. If we do not consciously identify the benefit and prioritize events like my mountain trip—or whatever that thing is for you—we are unlikely to put them on the calendar. A little effort in scheduling and priority on the front end opens up the space for possibility and potential for growth at the event itself. This takes engagement, as we discussed in the previous chapter, and reflection.

Once we have engaged, how did it make us feel? Once we reflect on these experiences, we can build a dataset of activities that we like, dislike, are fearful of, are excited about, or make us feel whole. These could be different for each person, and self-awareness is critical. It could be an interest, an activity, or even a philosophy. Some possibilities include misogi (a Japanese ritual of mental or physical challenge of self to promote growth), a meditation practice, a regular swim, a morning jog, weekly pickleball, or simply scheduled time to just sit and be. This chapter is focused on solo missions, but when identifying these nonnegotiables that we do for ourselves, we could also include an annual girls' weekend, a golf trip, or an annual destination event with a family member. Whether consciously or not, we prioritize, and subsequently allocate, our time, so where do we put ourselves on that list?

These expressions of engagement are markedly different from traditions. I recognize the value and pride that may be present in keeping our history and culture alive. Further, culture is essential to who we are as people, and traditions derived from culture can be life-giving and sacred. However, every single person reading this book either previously or currently has something in their life that they consistently do simply because it is what they have always done. No other reason than that. Who are we doing them for? Do we even ask? We often justify this repeated misery by saying we are doing this thing for someone else, who most likely doesn't want to continue the obligation either. I am guessing many of you are thinking of the holidays with family. (Hey, don't get mad at me. You were thinking it. I'm just saying it.) It doesn't mean we no longer love our family, or that we are miserable being around them. But we do tend to put an undue pressure on ourselves, stretch ourselves thin, argue, hold grudges, who knows what else, simply in the name of tradition! Is that useful? Is it healthy? Maybe sometimes, but I would venture to say, probably more often, it is not. We can each ask ourselves that question, and I encourage you to answer it honestly.

Sometimes something we do has a shelf life. Everything is not meant to serve us forever. If my annual retreat, which I mentioned at the beginning of the chapter, ever becomes an obligation, or is no longer fruitful, then it will come to an end. Not as a failure. An ending.

Said again differently, all things that end did not fail. What *would* be more of a failure would be to force it for years or decades to come, simply because I have told people how awesome it is, or because I have done it every year. "I have to continue to feel this way because I have always felt this way." NO! Doing so may very well be ignorance disguised as some sort of imagined noble consistency. This could be through traditions, relationships, social groups, or a vocation. Leaving one of these behind doesn't necessarily mean it was bad or wrong, and it does not have to be defended or justified.

Perhaps a relationship ended because growth and purpose began looking different for each partner, and for each to achieve what they wanted, it was most beneficial to move forward outside of that relationship. Or a relationship was sustained by redefining their goals to fit the present iteration of their partnership, shedding the aspects that no longer serve their collective vision, and courageously making changes through vulnerability and openness.

Maybe working for one company or in a particular career field created the financial means to make a career shift to pursue meaning, purpose, and passion. Was the first job wrong because it did not fit forever? Or did it hold significant value in contribution to a higher calling?

We are only able to adapt and evolve in a healthy way through self-reflection. While nonnegotiable events and experiences, such as my annual retreat in the mountains, are repeated patterns and behaviors, as seen in traditions, that is where the similarities stop. Unlike following tradition, this new, created experience is something reflected upon, in direct benefit to, and curated for, the self. Each person should identify their own, and give themselves the grace to change with time. The examples above show this can be done inside of a larger group than the self, but it must begin with the self.

Early in my career, I was talking with someone else in the industry when I was moving into a new role within my company. He did not ask me how much they were paying me, but he was adamant that I had a voice in the situation. The way he said it has stuck with me for years. "You have to look out for number one," he said, "or you end up stepping in number two." I use that quote often in conversation to remind others (and myself) the importance of caring for self. Self-compassion is not selfish. In fact, it is more the opposite. If we do not take care of ourselves first, we immediately lessen our value to others. Besides, if we do not actively care for ourselves, why would we expect anyone else to care for us?

Advancing your own time in solitude

The format of my second-week-in-January retreat has evolved over the years, and I am happy to share that format and what I aim to take away. The most important takeaway is making space in our lives to spend intentional time alone. Yours may not be a retreat in the mountains, and even if it is, it may look entirely different than mine. All are OK.

In actuality, I prefer not to call it a retreat. The idea of a retreat is to withdraw and take a step back from the distractions of our daily life. But when I think of the word retreat, I also think of running away. A defense mechanism to stave off or prolong defeat. I do not regard my time alone in the mountains of north Georgia like that at all. It is much more of a confrontation than a running away. An integration rather than a dichotomous interaction. A form of high connection rather than a disengagement. I appear to do less during this time, yet I always walk away with more. As ancient Chinese philosopher Lao Tzu said 2,500 years ago, "nature does not hurry, yet everything is accomplished."

There is a song called "Lochloosa" by JJ Grey where he expresses this feeling masterfully. He describes a rural place where there is a little boat on a pond with a fishing pole and an ice cold beverage at sunset. Someone suggests that he goes there to escape reality, and he acknowledges for a moment that could be true. But then he goes on to say that is not it at all, he says he goes there to *get* to reality. That is how I feel during my time in north Georgia, and it helps me to maintain a sense of calm and presence when I am not physically there in the still and quiet.

If not a *retreat*, what shall this retreat-sounding event be called? The direct opposition to retreat was most likely the initial draw to *advance*, and the term really grew on me. It implies a lack of stagnation, possibly even a hint of momentum in a desired direction. It is not a flashy word, not a rush or an erratic movement or a sneak attack. There is a healthy ambiguity to it. A reminder that advancing may look different for different people. Even within my example, what it means to advance could change its appearance from year to year. Finally, it symbolizes growth. Growth is subjective, and certainly not linear, but it speaks to a larger idea of purpose. Existential thought, meaning, and purpose are some of my favorite things to study and talk about, and we will dive deeper into those concepts throughout the book.

Although I nailed it with *advance,* I felt like that was not quite enough to describe the full essence. Advancement, growth, purpose, mountains, waterfalls. . . I began to think about what makes this so special. And I thought about this, by myself. Alone. I do this alone. I experience all of this, alone.

This helped me realize that the major component missing in the naming of my annual trip was solitude. It is important to note, being alone is quite different from being lonely. I have felt some of my moments of most connectedness in complete solitude. In contrast, I have been with groups of people and felt like I was on an uninhabited island in an ocean on another planet.

More time was probably spent on the naming of this thing than I would like to admit, but where it landed feels perfect. I have kept it private until this moment. So here and now I would like to formally introduce the Advance in Solitude.

Allow your process to evolve over time

The first year of the Advance, I didn't even know I was doing it. I had no huge plan, no intention to replicate, and no real expectation. And those factors all helped in making it so impactful. We certainly do not need all of the answers before we start. Most of the time, if we did have all of the answers up front, we probably would never start in lieu of a "better" solution. That is a slippery slope, because we can kick that can all the way down the road until we lose interest in can kicking. We are imperfect, we are human: start, go, do, be. We are all building our ship as it sails.

During that first year, I thought I was simply spending a weekend by myself in a little town I used to visit as a child. My maternal grandparents were born and raised there, and they had a small mountain cabin where we could stay in the summers. Between my Pa's nine siblings and their families, and my Nana's eight siblings and their families, I felt like I was related to the entire town. I am sure there were dynamics that I didn't see or understand, but my perception was that it was such a welcoming and familial atmosphere at all times. If we were not going to visit a great-uncle or some cousins, they were swinging by the mountain house unannounced. There was no need for announcement, because everyone was welcome, always.

The house was built on a hill, so the floor where you walked in became the second floor by the time you got to the back porch. We never noticed that the house was small or old. It had an unfinished basement that housed cobwebs, spare lumber, and other things with a heartbeat that I heard but never saw. But that back porch. . . It had a lean to it, sloping down at a slightly less pitch than the mountain, but no one ever seemed too concerned about that. It was deep enough to fit a little picnic table short ways, and if I had to guess, it was maybe sixteen feet long across the back of the house. But man, we would pile some people on that thing. It had the perfect view. Down below we could see the town and hear the passers by, and just beyond the town was a perfect view of Black Rock Mountain.

My Pa was a ham radio operator, and we would sit on that porch at night and listen to people place their orders at the McDonald's down below us in town. We had a close enough view to be able to see what type of vehicles were pulling into the drive-through, so we would guess their orders before they got up to the speaker.

By day, we could drive up to Black Rock Mountain, up the steep and winding road that could queue up a bout of car sickness in me by the first curve. But once at the top, it was all worth it. We would point out places around the town, people's houses, and even our little mountain house on the hill across the way. You could see out into the distance for what felt like a hundred miles.

All of my great aunts and uncles who were still in the area lived within a five-mile radius of the mountain house, seven at the most. We would go to one and have some fresh homemade biscuits and whatever type of jam was just made. Leave there and go play in a creek at another's house. I had my first-ever Spam sandwich at my great aunt Sally's house, which is something you kind of remember for a while. At some of the visits around town, we would just sit and listen. That seems like it would have been boring for an elementary or middle schooler, but that is certainly not how I remember it. I could listen for hours to all of the stories of lore, hard times, good times, living out in the country, and probably some lies depending on who was telling it. Never let the truth get in the way of a good story.

The memories of those times feel distant yet significant. The dates were never recorded, so the amount of times visited is a mystery. If impact were the best predictor, ten times per summer seems appropriate, however twice is likely more accurate. That's OK. I would rather the experience be an inch wide and a mile deep than the other way around. Needless to say, having the ability to spend quality time alone in a place with such pleasant associations is a bonus.

The second year of the Advance in Solitude, I am not even sure I consciously had the idea that this could be a thing. I think toward the end of that year I just began feeling like I needed to get away to reset and reboot, so I sort of just "went again." This feels really important to note, mostly for those of us who think we don't have it all figured out yet. At this point, I did not even know I was in the process of figuring anything out. We really don't need very many answers or certainties to start something. To act. To engage.

This trip, I once again stayed at an Airbnb, a different one this time than the first. This one was just outside of town nestled near the base of a small mountain. I had stayed there once before with a friend while in the area on a white water rafting trip. The structure had a simple, square footprint, maybe four hundred square feet inside, with a partially screened wrap around porch outside. The railing of the porch appeared to be handmade by hammer and nail with limbs possibly picked up from the property.

The interior of the little cabin was wood everywhere, some stained and some painted. There was an open room with a sitting area and a dining area that bled into the kitchen area. A door led to the only bedroom, and a ladder led up to a small loft above. The bathroom was not large but sufficient. On a tiny table just between the eating area and the kitchen area was some chocolate and a handwritten note welcoming me back to the place.

I don't really know exactly what it was about this place that made me so happy, but I just loved it. It was painted in green and burnt orange-ish, as was the shed that definitely used to be an outhouse, as well as the primary home on the property where the owners resided. It had a soft smell of what I remember kerosene to smell like, which maybe triggered a distant memory from my past that I was unable to recall. I believe what I liked the most was that it was in an area I loved, and was tucked so nicely in the private stillness of southern Appalachia. I felt like I was out there just living life as people have done right there on that hill for over a hundred years.

Some may call what I have described as roughing it, but it did not feel that way to me. That is, until I arrived right at dusk, with temperatures dropping heavily on what was a very cold night for this part of the world. The low was in the high twenties, and being from South Carolina, I was really excited at the rare opportunity to binge wear all of my jackets and hoodies over the next four to five days. What I did not know until I parked my truck and exited the vehicle, that I would shortly be very un-excited about, was that I would soon have the opportunity to wear them all at once under the covers that night.

There had been a winter storm that came through the area and all of the rain freezing on the tree branches and power lines had caused widespread power outages. Since this particular cabin was, now unfortunately, located in a remote part of the county, it was unlikely power would be restored any time soon. The owner of the cabin met me in the driveway. Apparently they had been trying to reach me for the better part of the day, but I had not checked my email, which housed the messages strongly suggesting I reconsider my trip.

The owners were incredibly nice, and offered me to come stay the night in their half-finished attic so that I would not get frostbite. He told me the other option was that he could go down to the house and bring me back a space heater to put in the bedroom, and between that and the blankets I might be able to get some rest. I chose option two, not wanting to impose on their residence. It had nothing to do with the fact that the movie *Deliverance* had been filmed on the Chattooga River just a few miles away.

When the owner returned with the space heater, I can only imagine the lack of ability I had to suppress my reaction. Or maybe I didn't even react at all, unable to effectively select the most present emotion. I don't know if I was more angry, wanted to laugh, or in fear that there was no way to maintain a livable body temp. I swear, if this heater was wrapped up for Christmas, every person reading this book would think it was a box of tissues. You know, the heater you put under your desk at work when the actual unit pumping out real heat throughout the whole building has you pretty comfortable, but you just want another little shot of warmth on your tootsies. They are not meant to heat a poorly insulated cabin in its entirety with an outside temp in the 20s.

I bundled up and made it through the night, and the heat was restored somewhere just before the sun rose. The rest of the trip went off without a hitch. Although at this point I still did not know this would become an annual occurrence, I did jot down notes throughout my time there. I went to some of my favorite hiking spots to waterfalls and overlooks, ate at my favorite restaurants, and spent time strumming my guitar.

By the three-year mark of the Advance, it finally dawned on me that it was becoming something beneficial that I really looked forward to. The few notes I took during the previous year were ideas, goals, and reflections that came out of the event, so I brought that back up as I entered the third year. Since it was now a streak, the decision was made to formalize it a little bit. Stress on the word "little," because I've wanted each year to take on a life of its own and develop organically. That said, some framework does certainly help to have an idea of what to do upon arrival rather than just stare at the wall for five days, and that evolved in due time.

Investing in your growth and managing distractions

Year three, and each subsequent year, of the Advance in Solitude has started with me selecting an intentional book that I aim to read in its entirety while I am there. Reading has been an incredibly important component of my life and has allowed me to grow in ways I previously did not realize. I believe that experience is the most valuable currency in the world, but if you are not able to experience people, places, cultures, and ideas by visiting them in the first person, then read books.

Read books that align with your views and beliefs. Read books that do not align with your view and beliefs. And do both with an open and curious mind.

Along with the intentionally selected book, I reflect on the list of books I have read over the past year. Which means throughout the year I note each book that I read and listen to upon completion. I also post that list to my social media on the last day of the Advance, and ask people to share book recommendations based on what has moved the needle for them recently. It ends up being a great way to engage with people in a valuable and meaningful way. It generates discussion about what has spoken to me through my reading list, allows me to make suggestions based on people's individual interests, and provides me with what typically becomes the majority of my upcoming year's reading list.

Part of this reflective and planning book process is goal setting, but in regard to reading, it can be a slippery slope to set a certain "number of books" goal for an upcoming year. Of course, it's helpful to have an idea of what we are working toward. It provides accountability and a reference point throughout the year to help keep us on track. The negative side, though, is becoming attached to the goal of the number, and *that* becoming the priority rather than the benefit of the content you're reading. I have been guilty of this and have found myself speeding through books just to meet my number. I include physical books, ebooks, and audiobooks in my overall count, and have caught myself just letting an audiobook run at times when I am clearly not digesting or retaining any of it. It is so easy to become distracted, and it takes constant focus and self-awareness to manage those distractions.

It should come as no shock that, in the 2020s, cell phone usage can still be a main distraction, when trying to spend intentional time alone. Limiting cell phone usage is a foundational component of the Advance. It seems like a dramatic change from daily life, and it certainly is, but there is also a natural separation from self and electronics as the proximity to mountains draws nearer. The feeling is pure refreshment, as the body physically feels the stress and anxiety dissipating. Your place might not be the mountains, though I don't understand how it couldn't be. But if you have a certain place that makes you feel different, go there. In going there and being vulnerable, open, and courageous, you just might be able to take that feeling with you and infuse it into all other areas of your life.

In a recent presentation on device and digital addiction, I was exploring the similarities and differences to substance addiction. Turns out, there are many more similarities than differences. Neurologically, genetically, and psychosocially, this type of behavioral addiction is very similar to a substance addiction. In addition, those with nonsubstance-related addictions are typically susceptible to increased substance use. Those with behavioral addictions also have an increased likelihood of depression and ADHD.

This is a relatively new area of study, specific to our devices, so the reported numbers I found in my research and provide below tend to vary and are not exact. My guess is that these are conservative numbers, and growing. Even if the numbers provided here were 20% lower, it would still be cause for concern.

The average person uses their phone about four and a half hours per day. We pick up our phones up to 144 times per day, which is about every six and a half minutes assuming sixteen waking hours. Does that sound like an addiction to you? Seventy-five percent admit to using their device while on the toilet. I mentioned this stat to a friend, and with a perplexed and confused look he asked, "what do the other twenty-five percent do?" That is where we are. Ninety percent of Americans say they check their phone within ten minutes of waking up. Imagine if that were meth, cocaine, or alcohol.

This type of addiction, similar to food and shopping addictions, are uniquely difficult because there is little to no expectation or possibility that people would stop. We will likely need, maybe even be required, to have a computer, phone, or tablet for our job and other areas of our lives. Because of this, it can become extremely difficult to manage.

All of these reasons make it imperative that I limit my cell phone usage during the Advance. I do not completely turn it off for five days, but I do significantly restrict usage. I leave it in airplane mode for most of the time. Any music, podcast, or audiobook that I potentially could listen to are all downloaded ahead of time. Pockets of phone time are pre-determined and discussed with family members.

Remember, this is my template. I encourage you to challenge yourself appropriately for your situation. I say "challenge" very intentionally, because it is important in this context to push yourself to do something you would not typically do. If you can go five days without looking at your phone once, that would be ideal. If you think you need to check in every hour, I would suggest beginning with the thought of no contact for the duration of your trip, and work backward from there. We are more capable than we think, and less important than we think. But also remember we are working through an addiction when it comes to our cell phone, so it will not be easy.

It's amazing how our expectations and actions change over time based on what is available. Humans are resilient and adaptable, which is a clear strength; however, sometimes we adapt in a nondesirable direction.

Alongside my friend Taylor Moss, I cohost The Constant Quest Podcast, where we explore authenticity, alignment, and growth. We also share conversations with guests who are able to share, each in their own way, their journeys of self-exploration, growth, and connection to a life of deeper meaning. In one episode, guest Matt Jaco shared that he had just returned from a six-week cross-country trip in a pull-behind camper with his family of five. Through his story, we highlighted how it is still possible to engage in adventurous and out-of-the-box trips with school-aged children with appropriate planning and intention. What was interesting, in the context of device usage, was hearing him compare his recent family trip to a similar trip he and his wife took twenty years prior.

During our episode, I asked Matt about the balance of being present in the moment with expectation of checking in back home with grandparents, work, and friends. Part of what made his trip a reality was his ability to use a mix of vacation days and remote work from the road, so finding that balance was crucial. He said they occasionally had difficulty finding services for a few hours when in Yellowstone National Park and other remote areas throughout that part of the country. He cherished this time, as his entire family was able to focus on being present in the moment and experience the day's activities together. He also acknowledged the pull of unfinished work obligations, sharing pictures with family, and checking in on the homefront.

Twenty years before this trip, Matt and his wife took a honeymoon camping road trip from Las Vegas to South Carolina. He said that they would go four to five days at times without sufficient cell service to check in with family. The difference was that no one knew what we know today, so there was no expectation to be strapped with connectivity at all times. Sadly, it makes me think about the thoughts that run through my head if I text someone and they don't respond in seven minutes or less.

So, when I am in the mountains for the Advance in Solitude, disconnecting from obligation, stress, and expectation is replaced with a full immersion in connecting to self, nature, reflection, creativity, and being. I designate a window of time twice per day to connect my cell phone with the rest of the world; otherwise, I am off grid. This process probably varies by person and situation, but it is crucial to push yourself and lean into the discomfort. Growth is found in discomfort.

I typically don't watch much television regardless, but I do make sure to limit that as well. I know my priorities going in, and that helps the decision-making process throughout the week. Perspective is an interesting influencer. I'm so excited about the ways that I am able to spend my time at the Advance that I do not really even consider replacing those things with watching TV, which I could do at any other time or place.

Each of you will find your own challenges. Some challenges you'll expect prior to an event like this, and some will surface in the moment. That does not mean you are doing something wrong. It's actually much more the opposite.

Reflecting and reintegrating

Each year, I write in my Notes app a list of impactful events as they occur in my life. It's not super formal, just a quick note to reflect back on later. I simply write the event or occurrence and the date. My favorite part about this process is that it can be unique to each individual. You are not being graded on this, and there is no right or wrong answer based on any external criteria. It can feel like a complement to filling out our calendars, as it allows us to reflect on how we actually feel once the days on the calendar have come and gone.

If you are willing to give this a try, please take ultimate freedom to record the types of things that feel significant to you. For me, they are vacations, races, surprise friend visits, concerts, catastrophic events, births, deaths, accomplishments, life changes. Things that feel significant.

It has been incredibly valuable each year at the Advance to reflect on the previous year. Sometimes we get caught up feeling like we have accomplished nothing or we haven't done anything significant simply because we didn't take time to remember and reflect. Doing so helps me feel a genuine, deeper level of connection to those who may have been involved in some of the experiences. It can clarify how we are spending our time and with whom. If you spend a great deal of time with someone who doesn't appear on this list of significant moments, it might be time to create some distance in that relationship. In contrast, there could be people who show up in several experiences you have deemed meaningful, but you do not allocate sufficient time and energy to those relationships.

The other component here is that when you do identify and realize that someone has positively impacted you, tell them. Tell them now. This might be my only exception to having my phone on airplane mode when I am spending intentional time alone. When I feel a sense of connection and gratitude for a specific person, it is of the utmost importance to me that I tell them immediately. Life is incredibly short, and we never know how many opportunities we have to tell those people dear to us exactly how important they are. Matter of fact, you can pause me. . . please take the time to text or call someone right now to let them know you are thinking of them.

Thank you.

Once I have gone through the past year's impactful events, I also reflect on the previous year's goals. I break down my goal setting into different categories. A great point of reference to use as a template when looking at ourselves as a complete person is called the eight dimensions of wellness. If you are not familiar with this concept, a quick Google search will provide a great visual. The eight dimensions in this model are: emotional, financial, occupational, physical, spiritual, social, intellectual, and environmental.

Each of these categories holds their own weight, and are co-dependent on the others, while all of these are connected to comprise an individual's overall well-being. I like to assign a number between one and ten to each category, to show my level of satisfaction. Ten being supremely satisfied with my current state within the given category, and zero being, well, the opposite of that. Assigning the number forces me to reflect intentionally, instead of using phrases like "oh, I'm doing all right in this area," or "I could probably use a little work here." The number makes it visible and real. It forces a decision and makes reflection (and measuring progress) easier within each area.

This is a good exercise to do periodically, as things certainly change over time. Kids are different ages, we value things differently, and time allocation inevitably changes. Looking at this once per year can show us an area or two where we would like to place a larger amount of focus in the upcoming months. We are also able to identify places where we feel like we are in a good spot.

The categories I use are slightly different from the eight I listed, because I believe it is important to focus on what we value. I include a category entirely for travel, because that is something that both my girlfriend, Nikki, and I regard highly. Over time, these categories should become reflective of what you value in your life, and they will bleed into one another. That is a good thing. Remember, these areas stand alone *and* are reliant on one another throughout the evolution of our self. It's validating when reflecting on a particular event or experience, and realizing it has impacted multiple dimensions. I consider that pro status.

The Dream-Goal-Process model is a large part of the Advance, where I plan for the upcoming year. The dream does not change a great deal over time, although it can certainly shift. Most of the time during the Advance is spent identifying goals in each category, and if time permits, building processes for each. I plan after reflecting, so that I am aware how certain experiences from the prior year made me feel. There are certain feelings we get in life that we yearn to replicate. Through reflection, vulnerability, and openness, I am better able to identify these experiences so that I am able to create the space for future opportunities to discover these desired feelings.

Although the benefits are immeasurable, if you are able to carve out a chunk of time to spend in complete solitude, it can be difficult to reintegrate. There might be a transition period when you feel uncomfortable as you begin to implement your reflections, ideas, and goals into your daily life. It might lead to tough conversations with loved ones and friends, perhaps even an unfamiliar awkwardness as you navigate prioritizing your values and dreams. It is all OK, and completely normal. It can be easy to retreat to what is familiar, but keep trying to listen to the inner guide, for it certainly knows you best.

Your inner guide has awakened, because you chose to do the work, because you engaged and spent intentional time alone. Learning, reflecting, growing. You've created a ripple effect that will touch every area of your life. What once was thought of as being selfish is actually a giant leap toward finding yourself, finding your people, and finding alignment.

Keep going.

Spend Intentional Time with Others

Both can be true

Spending intentional time with others may seem to be in direct opposition to spending time alone, but it's not. I often joke about writing a book called *Both Can Be True*, because I think we can sadly slip into an either/or mentality, when really it is both/and. In fact, for any one thing to reach high value, it is often in large part dependent on the other's mere existence. For instance, what is sunshine without rain? Light without darkness? Waking without sleep? Joy without pain? When we receive a sufficient amount of each, we may reach a state of homeostasis. One may not be in equal proportion to the other, but there is a level of balance.

I wonder why we often take on an all-or-nothing, one extreme or the other, approach. We either eat all meat or all vegetables. All Republican or all Democrat. Many times we stick with our extreme position over time simply because that has been our stance, so we must not waiver. I long for a society where there are respectful conversations about difficult topics, where one may say: "You appear to lean a little more liberal on this topic. I'm interested to hear your thoughts." Instead of, "oh, you're a Republican, F you, I hope you die." One way holds potential to become productive, or at a minimum non-violent, and the other way does not. There doesn't always have to be an "us vs. them" mentality. There actually doesn't even have to be a right and a wrong in each scenario. Some things simply are.

So, both things can be true. It can be incredibly valuable to spend intentional time alone *and* spend intentional time with others. Think about how old and stale things tend to become when we don't balance them out in some way.

One of the first times I learned about this "both can be true" ideology was through running. The local running store where I live, Strictly Running, has a 10 Commandments of Running that they live by. Two of those commandments are: Don't always run with others, and don't always run alone. I love that.

When I challenged myself to run a 5K every day for a month, I thought of these commandments often. At the beginning of the month, I was fired up and excited to be running each day as part of a larger goal. About a week in, though, it had already become something I felt I had to do. Like an obligation. I was still happy I was working toward a month of consecutive runs, but that initial excitement was waning. If the weather wasn't great, I would run them at the gym on a treadmill. Or if I couldn't squeeze one in throughout the day, I angrily ran around my neighborhood as fast as I could before bed. I was still getting my exercise, and that was a huge positive, but I wasn't enjoying it. Enter the commandments. I reached out to people, some whom I hadn't seen in a while, and asked them if they would like to go for a run. As I scheduled these buddy runs, I woke up joyful in anticipation of these interactions. So, I started calling more people, to the point where sometimes I had six or seven buddy runs in a week!

Simply adding friends and turning my runs into a time of fellowship and camaraderie changed the entire dynamic of my back-on-track run streak. As a byproduct, it also made my solo runs that much more special. After several buddy runs, I found myself looking forward to that time alone in thought. And vice versa, after a few days in my own head, I welcomed the opportunity to spend some time analyzing someone else's head.

Who pulls you up or pulls you down?

Notice I did not start with a story about me and a bunch of my home-boys bellied up at a bar screaming absurdities. I am certainly not here to say that phenomenal times can't be had at a bar with your boys, or girls, because I have had somewhere in the millions. But similarly to the previous realization, there is a difference between time spent with others and *intentional* time spent with others. While I would not trade my nights in Five Points drinking two dollar Beam and Cokes my entire college career for anything in the world, that is just not exactly what we are talking about here. Here, we are talking about engagement with others that cultivates growth.

I was going to talk about this later in the book, but this feels like an appropriate segue, so I will go ahead and take the bait. There is no replacement for true, lifelong, got-your-back-no-matter-what friends. There are people who know me better than anyone else ever will simply because of the things we have been through together. They know where I came from, who I was, and who I have always been.

There is also a point in life where we must realize that, in order to grow into the person we want to become and to live in full authenticity, our friends will begin to look different. It is true. Maybe sad, but definitely true.

That does not mean you've forgotten the people from your past. It doesn't even mean that you've cut ties with people from your past. It simply means that you have got to determine for yourself what your passions, interests, and beliefs are for *you*, and then surround yourself with people who have similar passions, interests, and beliefs. What are you interested in becoming? Who embodies those traits? Spend time with them. That is growth. That is growth before you even know you are growing, because you are watering a seed and exposing it to sunlight.

Once you start to make these shifts in approach, watch for the ripple effect in your life. You may see some of those long-term friends become inspired and take a similar route based on their interests and aspirations. It might not look the same as yours, but as an equally important contribution to the world. We don't need more of the same. We need more authenticity.

Support, collaboration, and accountability are important factors in our own personal growth and the growth of others. But approach these things with caution. It doesn't make you responsible for another person, nor does it make anyone else responsible for your growth. If you are continuously feeling pulled down, guilted, or shamed by someone close to you, separating yourself and setting boundaries is imperative.

This is a common challenge. Think of the crab in the bucket analogy. Fellow crabs might think they are protecting or saving you from the evils of the world by pulling you back into the depths of the bucket. Or, they know they have grown complacent, and the sight of your courage scares or angers them. Their fear and discomfort does not have to be yours. There is a great big ol' world just over the rim of that bucket, get out there and take a peek.

It's often difficult to identify who's helping and who's hurting. This is a gradual process that unfolds over time, but I bet there are some low-hanging fruit in your life that come to mind who aren't, in fact, fruitful at all. Separating yourself does not require a confrontation, a middle finger, or an I'm-better-than-you-so-there attitude. More the opposite, it requires courage to be a better version of yourself, for yourself. Trust your intuition, and make decisions with your time that best serve your growth and well-being.

Rapper, producer, and record executive Dr. Dre talks about this struggle throughout his career and how challenging it can be to tell the difference. He said the following in an interview with rapper Lil Wayne on Young Money Radio: "People are either pushing or pulling, and I wish I had known the difference early on in my career. I could've saved myself a lot of heartache in that area. At this point in my life, I see the value of surrounding myself with people who push me forward. I don't want to be around anyone I can't learn something from."

Who in your life pulls you down? Who pushes and propels you forward? Once you have identified both, think about how you currently allocate your time. Are you pleased with whom you are prioritizing your time? Life is short. . . choose wisely.

Going all in on your dream

In the summer of 2024, I drove a van across America and back. An incredible privilege it is to be in a position to turn that idea into a feasible possibility. I had dreamed of doing some version of this trip for years. As soon as I saw a small window of possibility and opportunity, I was all in. There were also strong doses of sacrifice, compromise, courage, and disregard for deep societal conditioning. I live in an area of the United States where society expects you to follow a certain path to be considered successful. My van trip went against those norms. As my friend Lester called it, I pushed the "fuck it" button.

I had been going to school at night as a full-time student working toward a master's degree in the mental health field, while also working full time in industrial sales. Near the end of my master's program, I moved into internship work, a forty-hour-per-week assignment—which meant my nearly twenty-year career in industrial sales, all with one company, would reach its end.

After a one-month break from school in May, I had a single class in June that was asynchronous, or self-paced online. I had intended on continuing to work during this time, so that I could save as much money as possible ahead of my upcoming, full-time, unpaid internship. That ended up not being the case. My company and I worked out that it made the most sense for all involved for me to leave at the end of March, four months earlier than I initially planned.

With the amazing support and encouragement of my girlfriend, Nikki, the trip became a reality. What I learned and experienced in that two months on the road could be an entire book on its own, and likely will be. But here we are talking about intentional time with others, so I will stick to that theme through the lens of this cross-country jaunt.

This was by nearly every definition and description a solo mission. An odyssey. A journey of personal exploration, internal dialog, individual growth, and self-discovery. One that I have longed to embark on for many years, inspired by the quest to feel free, all by myself, out on the open road. So, why are we talking about it in this section that should be all about interacting with other people? Remember when I said that time spent alone almost always involves other people, either directly or indirectly? Remember when I went for a run with other people, it yielded more positive experiences on my solo runs? That is why.

Throughout this trip, or VanAm as I call it, I felt deeper and richer experiences with those I interacted with along the way. Some in-person, others from a distance. Some were friends I have known for many years, others I met in-person for the first time. And countless complete strangers.

Many days, I would have five-plus hours of windshield time. Some of those hours were accompanied by pre-selected audiobooks and podcasts. Some were spent in silence, witnessing the passing landscape, allowing my imagination to drift and create and wander freely. Some hours were spent connecting over the phone with people who were closely following along from the life I left in South Carolina. They had some level of investment in my adventures and whereabouts, because they cared about me.

It's easier to say I was just talking shop with buddies while they were bored at work. There was gossip, shit-talking, travel recommendations, places I shouldn't have gone, concerns about money, life updates, stories of what I missed. But no matter the topic of conversation, I was just overwhelmed with appreciation and gratitude that someone I cared about was thinking of me. Everyone who checked in with me along the way was on the journey with me, whether they knew it or not. In large part due to those interactions, I experienced almost no loneliness throughout VanAm, though I spent well over a thousand hours alone.

In addition to those phone calls and texts, there were quite a few in-person friend visits at different points along the way. With only a general idea of a preferred route before setting off, I was able to plan many of my travel destinations around places where friends lived. That is a totally different type of interaction than a phone call.

Understandably, we cannot always drop in on friends who live states away, and a phone catch-up is certainly valuable. Sometimes we have so much going on that an hourlong phone call is not realistic, and we resort to a text exchange. That also holds value. Hell, at times it feels like it's the best we can do to keep up with our loved ones' whereabouts via social media, clicking the like button when and where we can to let them know we are still connected. All of those can be true, and they do still display a form of connection. And if that is the best or most we can do at a given time, we should still engage in that way, because any form of connection matters.

With that being said, the depth of a connection, or even of a single interaction, is largely dependent on our own investment. Our vulnerability, effort, and level of engagement. Fairly often I field comments from friends about the number of different people I interact with. People from all walks of life, different professional backgrounds, areas of interest, ages, and geographies. Often those comments feel like they are offered as an insult. "We all can't be as lucky as you," or "of course you know someone that works in that field."

First, I will say that I am incredibly lucky. I have a support system and network unlike anything I could have ever dreamed of. People show up for me again and again, no matter what. Also worth mentioning: I work really, really hard at it. I show up. I check in. I try to ask meaningful questions, and I make an effort to support people in what is important to them. And the reciprocation is felt. This is not meant to toot my own horn, but it must be illustrated that meaningful relationships don't just pop up out of thin air.

So, when I reached out to these friends scattered across America in a randomly perfect constellation of travel stops, it was well-received. There seemed to be a mutual excitement for each of these visits. Sure, there was sacrifice and compromise in every case—missed work time, child care, routine disruption, financial implications—but that didn't deter me. That made me appreciate them more. It made our interactions that much more special.

Why do we back out of things at the first whiff of inconvenience? Also, why are we uncomfortable when someone prioritizes time with us? It's an incredible compliment, one that we should accept with open arms. Frequently, I hear someone talking a person out of a compliment or a nice gesture. I, too, have been guilty. Generally, we are poor at taking compliments and acts of kindness. When someone does something nice for you, it takes some amount of vulnerability. How do you think it is received when we brush it off like it is nothing? It's not nothing, it's a big deal, and we should let them know that. We can also get caught up trying to out-nice each other that we miss out on the possibility of something amazing.

Due to the nature of making a cross-country road trip, it didn't work out where I could see every person when it was convenient for them. Some were mid-week, late at night, early in the morning, on a day someone's child had a game, when someone was scheduled to work. And every single one of them made it happen. Multiple people took days off of work to spend time with me. Can you imagine how much more valuable that time with them became? Oftentimes when we just do what is convenient for everyone, it waters down the experience. Every person I visited made a sacrifice of some sort, and I did not feel guilty. I felt grateful.

Several people invited me to stay in their home, which was a nice breather from sleeping in the van. I was prepared home-cooked meals, taken to favorite restaurants, given parting gifts for my travels ahead. One friend actually got on a plane and flew to a different spot in their region because of some logistical challenges that arose in our schedules. Instead of her being able to show me around her city, which would have been special, we shared a hike through Zion National Park, one of the most majestic places on earth. Incredible! She easily could have said, "hate I missed you, catch you some other time." But she didn't. This stuff matters. I went to a show at Red Rocks, took a yoga class, went to a major league baseball game, hikes, runs, walks, bike rides. I even made an appearance at one of my friend's family reunions.

More than all of those things, what will be remembered and revered most are the conversations born through those experiences. When I say to spend intentional time with others, this is exactly what I am talking about. Through the willingness of so many people to make an effort and a sacrifice, a shared experience was created that we now have forever. They became a part of my journey, too. They poured into me, and I was able to share my experience with them.

Then there were the complete strangers. Maybe there is something about the vacation effect that makes someone more willing and open to striking up random conversations with complete strangers. I am extremely extroverted, so not a huge jump for me, but even I did feel an added level of comfort and confidence jumping right in. There was an understood justification, and permission was granted. I'm not entirely sure why that is, but I have made an ongoing effort to carry that with me wherever I am. We never know what could come of an interaction with a stranger.

To highlight the meaningful interactions and conversations with strangers over the two-month course of VanAm would take several chapters. There were far too many to count, and they came in all shapes and sizes. There feels like an open understanding, in places like National Parks, to engage with passersby and fellow park goers. Actually, that is a large part of the experience in parks. Sharing an adventure, a hike, or a beef stick on a rock on the side of a mountain. There were rides on just about every form of transportation imaginable: bus, shuttle, boats of varying size and speed, train, gondola. Each an opportunity to pass the time with someone on an adventure of their own. It is fascinating to just sit and listen to people's stories. Of course, there were plenty of opportunities to share my own, and I was excited to do so, but we all have a story to tell. If you want to see someone light up and engage, ask them about themselves. It's not always about us.

The park interactions led to meeting people from all over the world. Families, retirees, group trips, bucket lists, and so on. Several conversations led to future stops on my own itinerary. Who better to take recommendations from than the people out there pounding the pavement and visiting places? I visited several places I hadn't previously heard of solely because of a two-minute conversation on a trail somewhere.

The other strangers I interacted with were those whom I witnessed right in the throes of their everyday life. The people who lived in the towns and cities that made up the blueprint of VanAm. Being able to witness daily life in such diverse geographies, demographics, and landscapes within my own country was a unique experience, and hearing the voices of the people inhabiting each of those places was impactful.

It may be common to poor-mouth our own town, and maybe it's in the vein of "I can talk shit about this place because I live here, but I better not hear you utter one foul syllable about it!" But this felt different. Maybe all the negative talk is reserved only for other people that live in the same place, a sort of shared misery. Or maybe this was just my experience, and it was atypical. But I was particularly overwhelmed by the level of pride that people displayed for the places they called home. I struggle to remember a conversation that left me feeling like I should have skipped the place altogether.

What I encountered was people who could not wait to brag about their community. Most started with food and social recommendations, many of which I obliged. Then their shares typically grew into what their area was known for, historical significance, and must-sees, accompanied with a list of reasons why. If I engaged long enough, many of these conversations led to a proud citizen turning their nose at wherever I intended to visit next, followed by another list of reasons why not. Perhaps it shouldn't come as a shock when people love the place they live, because they did decide to live there, or at the very least, haven't decided yet to leave. But I didn't expect it.

I felt genuine deflation when breaking the news to people that I was only passing through for a day or two. It turns out that is not near enough time to explore every single place in America. Surely there is some truth to that, especially if we allow ourselves to engage.

Finally, when it comes to intentional time with others on my VanAm haul, the glaring omission so far is the mention of my girlfriend, Nikki. My intention of holding this part until the end of this chapter was to first illustrate that you can go and do amazing things on your own. You can create your own experiences, and interactions, and random, rich relationships all by yourself. There were years of my life when I was single that I thought I was inadequate or incomplete, so I passed up on countless opportunities to engage. So, for anyone sitting around sad because they don't have anyone to go on an adventure with. . . GO ANYWAY. There are so many incredible conversations, relationships, and interactions to be had, but first, you have got to walk out the door.

Now for the flip side of this: You *can* go and do amazing things if you are in a relationship. Both with your partner, and with their support from afar. There are many people who have a partner and feel like they cannot experience what I have described above, at any scale. That makes me sad. This is not a relationship column, and I'm certainly not one to offer advice as if I have it all figured out, because I certainly don't. I just know that, at the end of the day, we are all still individuals. When we support and encourage that uniqueness and authenticity in a partner, the strength of the union is often a benefactor.

I am blessed beyond measure to have such support from Nikki, and although I probably come up short, I make every attempt to reciprocate. VanAm would not have been a possibility without her unwavering support. My ability to dive in head first and engage with myself and others the way that I did for an extended period of time was only made possible by her selflessness, understanding, and encouragement.

Earlier, when I talked about solo time involving more than one person, this type of situation firmly qualifies. It was not easy. We each had our own emotions, expectations, and fears. Certainly we were both excited, and we were also scared and nervous. For similar reasons, and for our own different reasons. Both of our lives would look completely different. And just like the friend visits I mentioned, in which both parties had to be vulnerable and put forth effort, we each had to commit. I have learned so much about taking on a supporter role for others from Nikki. It is hard work. And the reward can be huge.

Nikki dove in head first as well, and helped where it was most useful to me. She reserved some of my campsites on long driving days. She watched weather systems all across regions of the country where I would be driving. She checked park closures and hours of operation. She celebrated with me when I had a moving and meaningful experience, and she cried with me when I was emotional. She always answered the phone when I needed a companion, and she willingly gave me space when I was looking inward and in solitude. None of those things were planned. There was no schedule for my emotional roller coaster. She hopped on and off with no notice, and always at the perfect time. She made it look so easy, and what probably means the most is that I know it was excruciatingly difficult for her at times. I never saw it or heard it in her voice, but I know it.

The day I left for VanAm, Nikki and I talked briefly about the difficult times. Not to harp on them, or create them by talking them into existence, but to assure each other that we were both there in the event of any challenging moment. She pulled out a card to give to me. There was a hand-drawn image on a piece of construction paper. In the lower right corner was her in bed under a palmetto tree by the lake where we live. On the left side was me wearing a flatbill hat, driving a van up a mountain. There was a dotted line connecting us to a moon at the top of the card. She told me that we wouldn't actually be apart because we would both be looking at the same moon each night. The back side had a hand written quote by Rumi: "Goodbyes are only for those who love with their eyes. Because for those who love with their heart and soul there is no such thing as separation."

Maybe I am making it sound like I was going away to war, or to circumnavigate the globe by ship in the fifteenth century. I don't want to overexaggerate the magnitude of the trip. But her thoughtfulness and intention with that gesture certainly deepened our connection. It helped fuel me through the first leg of VanAm across the country, which ironically, is when I would see her next.

The second part of this is that Nikki was able to fly to meet me for a small portion of the trip. After driving across the country and making a few friend visits, I picked her up in Las Vegas to join on the Pacific leg of the trip. We had a list of things we would like to try to see, but very little scheduled other than Spartan races. We had a Spartan Beast at the site of a ski slope in Big Bear Lake, California, and exactly two weeks later another one in Bozeman, Montana. The space in between was ours to explore. We did visit people in that two-week span as well, all of whom were incredibly flexible with our inexact schedule.

Along with the excitement and anticipation of her arrival was the necessity to adapt. After I learned to exist on the road alone for a couple of weeks, her joining me did change the entire dynamic. Not in a bad way. It just all of a sudden looked different. For example, we doubled the number of people living inside of a van. If you long to discover if you and your partner are actually even friends, may I recommend living in a van while travelling. It is like all the stressors of relationships, occurring simultaneously. Travel, constant decision making, what to eat, where to eat, spending money on atypical things, no personal space, extreme weather, uncertainty. And they are all occurring inside of a 2500 Ford Transit Van that can fit in a regular parking spot.

I have found it beneficial to put a relationship to the test. It's helpful to know how each other responds in tense moments when a challenge arises. This environment breeds vulnerability, another crucial element in a relationship. It creates a unique bonding experience that is difficult to manufacture when we are just going through the motions or on auto-pilot. It is important to protect each other, as well as to push and challenge each other. Would you avoid this situation like the Covid? Or would you lean into it with excitement of the potential to grow? To deepen a connection, to learn more about yourself and your partner. To figure out what you are made of, only to realize you could be made of even more!

You don't really even have to drive across America in a van to experience what I am talking about, which is spending intentional time with your partner. Being intentional with the conversations you have, the questions you ask, and carving out and prioritizing time to be spent together. There is a lot of fear in this: fear of change, fear of an answer we don't want, fear of inadequacy, fear of not measuring up to all of the other "perfect" couples on social media.

Insert any of the thousand great quotes on fear. There are thousands of them because we all have it. And if we are lucky, like the authors of many of the quotes, we get to experience glimpses of what the other side of fear looks like. There are many different angles and takes on fear, but what has resonated with me the most lately is how Elizabeth Gilbert describes it in her book *Big Magic.* She says, and I'm paraphrasing, that fear is always there, and that is OK. Fear can come along for the ride; it just cannot drive.

That really speaks to me, specifically in regard to partnerships. Although we feel like we know our partner better than anyone, and vice versa, it can be the most difficult to continue to be vulnerable with them over time. Vulnerability is not a one-and-done thing. Have you ever found it oddly easy to spill your guts to a complete stranger? It's easy because they don't know any other version of you. You can freely unload your present thoughts and feelings without any real expectation. It's the therapy effect. We feel like we have permission to be ourselves. Do you feel like that with your partner? Does your partner feel that level of comfort with you? What steps can you take right now to help create an environment that fosters vulnerability, openness, and authenticity? It can be very hard, and very scary. And yet, beauty lies on the other side.

It may be easier if you're able to interrupt the typical cycle of your relationship. Try doing something spontaneous, out of the ordinary, whatever that looks like in your specific situation. That was my experience with Nikki living in the van for a couple of weeks. I won't speak for her, but I felt a level of freedom, openness, and vulnerability through our time on the road. We intentionally removed ourselves from our normal environment, and were creating something new, together.

We now have dozens of shared experiences, adventures, and stories that we otherwise would not have had. And we have them forever. We were able to see and do some really incredible things in her sixteen-day stint. She really leaned into what had become my routine on the road. How and when to put up the van shades, exactly where to store certain things in our now tinier space, how to address tooth brushing, showering, and using the bathroom.

In just her two short weeks, along with the two Spartan races, Nikki and I spent time with four friends and visited seven national parks, spanning nearly three thousand miles. It was a marathon and a sprint. I learned a lot about her and from her through that time together. Her positivity and optimism helped balance my increased anxiety from wanting to make her experience perfect. She somehow perfected this dual role of co-creator of our part together and supporter of my larger masterpiece. She never showed an ounce of resentment toward my being able to do considerably more. That had to be very difficult for her, because she certainly wanted to join, but she decided to take the route of full engagement of the time she did have. And due to that, we discovered depths of our relationship previously uncharted. How does the saying go? Everyone should get themselves a Nikki—you just can't have my Nikki.

Having these types of experiences together only open up the possibility for more in the future. As said previously, vulnerability isn't one and done. It's a muscle that we continue to build and exercise. If we stop using it, it will atrophy. Lean in with intention, and reap the rewards.

Engage to find your community

When I think of spending intentional time with others, I now think of the word "community." For the majority of my life, I'm not sure I knew what this word really meant. What it did mean to me is a far cry from what it has become. My town had a community center, so one association with the word was that it was a structure, a building. When applying for jobs and creating a resume, it seemed important to include something about community engagement or service. So, in that context, it was probably defined by me as fluff, or possibly even felt as an obligation. A small town could be called a community, so another definition could be a geographical area.

None of those, even combined, come close to encapsulating what community has come to mean to me. At the beginning of this section, we talked about how friends and social circles might look different as we grow and evolve. It doesn't have to be a replacement for childhood friends, although it could be. Think of it more as expansion. It tends to take care of itself when we are more intentional.

You may have heard college coaches, in pretty much every sport, say something like, "the numbers always work themselves out." Whether it be scholarship allocation, necessary cuts, or transfers, when it's time to tee it up, toe the line, kickoff, face off, or tip off, somehow the numbers have fallen into line. It falls into line because it's the utmost priority for a coaching staff. First, they must identify what type of players they want on their team. What type of body language do they have? How do they carry themselves, how do they react in the face of adversity? What skill sets fit into what would help the team move in the direction of the desired outcome? They don't just show up to the first practice and figure it out with whoever showed up. They are intentional about the type of team they are building. It's tough to build community without identifying the type of people by which we would like to be surrounded.

Coaches spend a great deal of their time and energy working on getting the right pieces in place. Not the most players, or the same type of players, but the right players who give them the best opportunity to be successful within their system. Players who offer their own unique skill set. Do you prioritize the right type of people in your circle? Are you interested in adding your blind spots, people who can help expand your skill set?

Of course, each coach wants talent. That is a large part of the equation, but it takes more than that. In basketball, what if you had an entire team full of point guards? All talented perhaps, but who is going to post up? Who is going to bang around in the paint and fight for rebounds? Does the makeup of your group look the same? How do you introduce new ideas and outside perspectives if everyone is the same? Do the skill sets of your team compliment each other?

Team chemistry is one of coaches' biggest challenges and unknowns from year to year. It's difficult to predict how people will gel with each other. Typically, early in a season, many different line-ups will be explored on a basketball team so that the coaching staff can determine who plays well together. This is much more than talent, and you never see a championship team that lacks chemistry. Have the players who receive little to no playing time accepted their role within the organization? Are they invested in the overall success of the team, and ready when their number is called? Do the most talented players buy into the team concept and become even better because of their supporting cast rather than performing in spite of them?

Some coaches have the philosophy to shoot a bunch of three pointers and rarely utilize a true post player. Does that mean a talented true post player is not any good and has no value? Absolutely not, but he could be on the wrong team. Are you on the right team? Have you surrounded yourself with people that are moving in a similar direction, with a similar philosophy? If your current friend group values different things, that's OK. You can still support them from afar. You just belong on a different team, with people who align with your dreams, have shared goals, and push you to be the best version of yourself.

In my current view of community, I find it's important to surround myself with like-minded people who make me want to strive to be the best version of myself, while also not creating a silo or echo chamber. This can be a fine line, and very difficult to balance. This is where understanding what we value becomes useful. My ideal community values growth, support, focus on physical and mental health, collective well-being, and stepping outside of our comfort zone. It also values openness, empathy, and curiosity. How do we cultivate growth if we are not open and curious about new and different ideas?

Once you have identified the type of people, ideas, and beliefs you want to build community with, it is time to put yourself in an environment where those things exist. You likely won't just open door number two and seamlessly fall right in line with a whole new group of people. But, you should still open door number two if door number one isn't serving you.

Put yourself in places where you'd like to see yourself. This sounds obvious, but it's so easy to fall into a cycle of doing the same thing over and over again. I used to say, "I don't really want to meet my girlfriend in a bar," and then I'd spend my time in bars. What did I foresee happening? Did it ever occur to me that my future partner also may not have wanted to meet their boyfriend in a bar? That's not to say you should not meet your partner in a bar. I've met many brilliant and amazing people there. I did not want to meet my girlfriend in a bar because I knew who I was in that environment. I had no self control, no "off switch." There were not many instances where I was capable of having an intelligent conversation in a bar. Certainly nothing close to a sober conversation. I had to remove myself from that environment. At minimum, I had to also exist in other environments where I found inspiration and positive influence. It took many many many years to understand this, and realized that I might even have to tread this new path alone at first.

Surround yourself with other people doing amazing things

What do you enjoy doing? What did you enjoy doing when you were younger? If you have a partner, what is a shared interest you have? Do you love jam bands? Enjoy theater? Cycling? Adventure traveling?

My friends Marty and Jeff love going to jam band shows. Initially they followed the String Cheese Incident pretty closely. And by closely I mean they have been to hundreds of shows spanning twenty years. All over the country, and even into other countries. That is something they enjoy, and they have met countless people doing just that. They now follow Billy Strings, and travel to see him with people that they have met by simply showing up and going to shows. By being open to creating community with people that have shared interests. They have traveled the nation and beyond with these people!

A couple in my hometown was recently in a musical theater production together. It started out several years ago with an interest. The husband had a passion for theater so he began showing up. Eventually he began helping out. He took on roles behind the curtain: sound, lighting, props. I just saw a video of him featured on center stage singing, and his wife on the stage singing with him! They have built community. Oh, and did I mention this all started when they were in their sixties?

My partner Nikki and I essentially met through our shared interest in running. Not in a bar, for those keeping score at home. If she ever knew that version of me, none of this ever would have happened. Again, not because of the bar, but because of the way I conducted myself in said bars. By the time we met each other, we had both shown considerable growth from former versions of ourselves, something I hope to continue until the day I die. Growth is one of our shared interests. Another is running. A mutual friend (Nikki's cousin) introduced us when she realized we had been attending and running many of the same events. Much of our initial relationship growth occurred while logging miles together on trails in the forest and along river walks. I am pretty sure our first three overnights were all out-of-town races that we attended together, citing efficient travel and reduced expenditures.

We shared other interests, such as travel, interacting with people, live music, and improving our overall health. A couple of years into our relationship, we each saw an ad on Instagram for an event called Runningman, a festival with music, sauna, cold plunge, speakers, and food trucks. And it was a running event. A one-mile horse track would become the running course on Saturday, and we could run it however many times we wanted in an eight-hour window. Before I even clicked on the ad, I took a screenshot and sent it to Nikki, and we were both in. This comprised most of the things we both love, all occurring simultaneously. I'm sure she did because she is more responsible than me, but I didn't look at the cost, the location, or the date. I didn't care. I was going.

The event was being put on, in part, by this guy called Jesse Itzler. I was familiar with him through a book he had written about a decade before. I stumbled across his book after I had read *Can't Hurt Me* by David Goggins. Heavy in my Goggins era, a friend told me there was a book about him living with some guy and his wife for a month. Originally only there for more Goggins content, I found that this guy Jesse grew on me. He was an incredible storyteller, and I flew through the book in no time. Not that I needed any more of a reason to attend Runningman, but it was pretty cool that he was one of the masterminds behind it.

The event itself was incredible. There were booths set up offering all sorts of health and wellness products and services. There were panel speakers that were already influences of mine. Different workshops throughout the festival were masterclasses on a range of topics. The run was an electric environment. Everyone was out there running around that one-mile loop together, whether running a 50K or a 5K. There was so much support and encouragement. During the run, the sauna and cold plunge area was open as well. We talked about the dimensions of wellness earlier as part of the Advance in Solitude, and expert level was being in situations where more than one dimension is present. Runningman offered many of the dimensions at once.

When I think of the type of community I want to be a part of, Runningman is at the top of the list. And the best part about it is that it does not stop there. We have now attended Runningman three years in a row, and have met some incredible people. I got involved in a Roundtable coaching group with Jesse, and continued to grow my network of like-minded people. Through these events, I have been asked to be a guest on podcasts and have met several folks that have been a guest on my podcast, The Constant Quest. I received great support from this community on my VanAm trip across America, when I did not feel like I received the same type of support locally. One of the stops actually ended up being to see a friend that I met through the Roundtable. We shared a run together in his hometown of Des Moines, Iowa.

Nikki ran forty-five miles in one day on her forty-fifth birthday to raise money and awareness for those impacted by hurricane Helene in Asheville and western North Carolina. The money went directly to Be-Loved Asheville, an incredible organization that has been working with the community for many years offering homes, building supplies, and other resources to underserved populations. They have taken on a monstrous role in hurricane relief, becoming a hub of donation and distribution throughout the region. Seeing their work firsthand in an area of such critical need has been incredibly impactful for both me and Nikki. One of the people who helped make Nikki's connection to BeLoved possible is someone we know through Runningman.

When Nikki first mentioned to me the idea of running forty-five miles for BeLoved, I remember being incredibly inspired. She told me that she wanted to help in any way she could, for a place that she has always loved. She loves to run, loves to challenge herself, and is the best supporter of others. We had recently followed along a guy who ran over eight hundred miles across Texas in under a month. We had watched this same guy win a pickle-eating contest at Runningman. We followed Harvey Lewis as he ran a world best four hundred fifty miles to win a last man standing endurance event, outdoing his previous year's total by seventy-five miles. We had never even heard of Harvey until sharing laps with him at Runningman. Another person we met, along with two others, raised $30,000 for multiple sclerosis by running the New York City Marathon.

It was incredible to be a small part of Nikki's huge accomplishment. It was something she created, trained for, and knocked out of the park. It also created a ripple effect felt by others in her life. Without question, part of her influence and inspiration was from the ripples of the others just mentioned.

Here is a formula, if you want to do amazing shit: Surround yourself with other people doing amazing shit. It is contagious. That is the power of community. And it comes from spending intentional time with others.

Be Present,
Be Mindful,
Meditate

Presence balances achievement

This section on being present could easily have been first in the book. Without the ability to be present, it may be difficult to feel any significant impact of engaging and spending time alone or with others. However, waiting for perceived perfect presence and alignment to exist before proceeding could very well impede forward motion and growth. If it is true that we are all figuring it out as we go, which I wholeheartedly believe to be the case, then another way of saying that is we have to "go" in order to figure it out. Therefore, engagement and intention landed ahead of presence in this book.

Presence is very much a practice, a muscle that we build over time with repetition. Therefore, engagement with nature, self, and others may be a big playground for presence to be practiced. They are not mutually exclusive. One does not need to master presence to then engage, nor the other way around. They may occur simultaneously.

Where engagement and intentional action can be seen as *doing*, presence balances that out with a focus on *being*. We are not trying to DO presence, we are aiming to BE present. Right here, right now. How often do we get caught up focusing on some future moment that we lose the ability to engage in whatever is going on right in front of our eyes?

There are similarities with presence, engagement, and intention. Here, we regard presence as another level of growth within the foundation being built. Growth is not linear, and the first few realizations in this book are not prerequisites to practice being present. Please use any of these realizations freely as they are useful to you.

Spending an entire section on presence, mindfulness, and meditation helps to balance out the metric-driven, insatiable hunger of competition and individual achievement that consumes much of our focus. It is difficult to gauge the impact of these practices, which can be frustrating and deterring. We want results, and they are often subtle, and at times seemingly invisible. But they are most certainly there.

There was a tagline that BASF used in their commercials in the 1990s and early 2000s that said, "we don't make a lot of the products you buy, we make a lot of the products you buy better." No comment on those products BASF claimed to be enhancing, but that line itself is how I feel about the practices of presence, mindfulness, and meditation. The environments and relationships we are engaging in already have the potential to become deeper, richer, and more impactful through these practices.

Another metaphor I often use to describe engaging in a meditative practice is, once again, a sports analogy, this one focused around football. For this example, we will use a D1 freshman quarterback. The number of quarterbacks at this level who garner playing time are few and far between. They were dominant in high school, and obviously have the skill to play at the next level. Of course, D1 college defenses are bigger, stronger, and faster than former high school opponents, but it is still the same game. The center still snaps the ball to the QB, the wide receivers still run routes, and the QB still throws them the ball. Along with skill development, strengthening, and conditioning, there is another intangible component to the quarterback's readiness that coaches often speak about. You will hear a coach say about a player, a quarterback in this example, "the game has really slowed down for them." The game is not being played any slower. The defense certainly isn't pulling back and making it any easier. But the quarterback is not thinking as much. They have practiced to the point where the routes and defenses have moved almost to their subconscious. They experience the whole picture in a flow state without having to analyze each tedious component in the moment. They don't hesitate, they don't overthink, they just play.

That is the feeling that I began to realize in my own life by meditating. I did not feel like I was in the backfield running for my life. Before, I had felt like I was chasing each day, trying to catch up and find my place in it, disheveled and rushing to every destination. With meditation, I began feeling like, when I walked out the door in the morning, I was right where I was supposed to be. The world slowed down. I was present.

It makes me think of the well-known Zen Buddhist saying: "Before enlightenment, chop wood, carry water. After enlightenment, chop wood, carry water." Once we build a process that we believe in, and realize it has helped us reach a state of enlightenment, joy, or contentment, we must then continue to engage in that process. The process we develop is the vessel in which we move through life.

Nelson Mandela said, "after climbing a great hill, one only finds that there are many more hills to climb." We are all climbing great hills, mountains even, and how are you climbing yours? With what process? One that breeds resistance, resentment, and disregard for the beauty of the path? Or are you enjoying the view? Are you joyful, content, aligned, and present? We cannot always prepare the path for ourselves, however we are more than capable of preparing ourselves for the path.

It might seem as though I use the words presence, mindfulness, and meditation interchangeably. That is not because I believe them to have the same meaning. Rather my discovery and initial understanding of all of them came in close proximity to each other. A time where I began feeling a shift in how I perceived the world around me, and the way that I existed within it.

On mindful, micro goal-setting

Doing a 5K every day for a month was part of what ended up being a much larger exercise of discipline, focus, and presence. Meditation became a part of this project as well.

I began thinking of this idea as "micro goal-setting," which I first heard about from a podcast episode that wasn't about goal-setting at all. It spoke about micro-adventures: quick, accessible activities we can participate in locally without having to plan, financially or logistically, for a huge trip.

I applied this logic to goal-setting as a way to give ourselves something more manageable than a year-long goal or a huge, drastic, overwhelming change. A month is long enough to create a habit, *and* short enough that we can see the light at the end of the tunnel. So, the month after I committed to running a 5K every day for a month, I set another micro-goal for myself: to meditate for at least ten minutes every day for one month.

If this process interests you, I encourage you to check out a series of articles I wrote on my blog, Tine Thinks, about this eighteen-month project of micro goal-setting. It changed my entire routine, which changed my habits, which changed the trajectory of my life. The articles cover the set of criteria used to determine each monthly task, how I recorded and reported outcomes, and the exact process and reflections from many of the individual months. Each article had the purpose and reasoning for choosing the goal, and then areas of growth realized after reflecting on the month.

The following is an excerpt from one of the articles I wrote after spending a month where I challenged myself to meditate for at least ten minutes per day.

Purpose

I have found myself continuously engaging in conversation about the idea that we should spend more time alone in thought. That's something I haven't always been great at doing. Now, that isn't necessarily what it means to meditate but those conversations with friends were catalysts that would eventually get me there. Only over the past couple of years have I become comfortable completing normal daily tasks by myself: getting gas, eating out, exercising, etc. So, if spending time alone WITH distraction was difficult, I certainly had never considered being alone and present in a given moment, undistracted.

One of my favorite singer/songwriters is Mike Posner, and I recently read that he had gone to a monastery in Colorado and spent an entire week in solitude. I was immediately intrigued. I began imagining what it would be like if I were to do something like that, if only for a weekend. How would I know who won football games? What if one of my customers had an emergency? How would I know what "everyone else" was doing? How would my mom know that I was OK? What if something happened?

As these questions floated through my head, I grew increasingly saddened. Saddened that we have gotten to a point where we are unable to take ten minutes out of our day for ourselves, let alone an entire weekend. So, I decided to set a goal of meditating for thirty consecutive days. That felt like a good place to start. The more I talked about this goal, the more I realized it wasn't as "weird" as I thought. I have several friends that have had good experiences that further encouraged me to try it out. Also, one of my favorite podcasts is The Tim Ferriss Show, where he interviews top performers in their respective fields and deconstructs their routines in an attempt to discover what makes them successful. The overwhelming majority of his guests practice some sort of meditative routine. I could have just started with that, because that by itself was enough for me to give it a shot!

Growth

I've been fortunate to have had the opportunity to take several eight- to ten-day trips to Central and South America. Some for fun, some to volunteer, but all as an opportunity to experience personal growth. In each of these trips I have found a commonality that is difficult to describe. It's not a specific thing, interaction, or physical being. It's a feeling. A calming, peaceful feeling where life simultaneously becomes simpler and more full. Where I am thousands of miles from those I love, but intimately connected with what it means to love. I've always found it odd that I only have that feeling when I'm on one of these trips. Why is it tied to specific geographies?

After a full month of practicing meditation, I am beginning to realize it is not based on geography at all. It is a mind state. By practicing being present in each moment it has simplified my daily routine greatly. It's helped me approach previously difficult situations with a calmness and focus that I hadn't before been able to achieve. It's helped to reduce anxiety, frustration, and clutter in my daily life. It has taught me to acknowledge and appreciate my current state of being mentally, emotionally, and physically. No longer constantly concerned with where I was five years ago, or where I'll be in five years, but where I am right at this moment. Man, life is such a blessing.

This reminds me of a time a few years back when attending a good friend's wedding in Charleston. On a table at their reception there was a large framed map of the world, and each person was to write their name on a tiny flag and pin it on their favorite place, wherever it may be.

My friend, who is from the US, works for a company based in Germany, and his wife is from Japan, so it was interesting to see flags scattered all across the map, many in places I had never even heard of. I waited until later in the evening to place my flag so I could scope out all of the places people had selected, thinking I may find a place to take my next adventure.

As I put my flag on Copacabana, Bolivia, a picturesque town in the Andes mountains that sits on the highest navigable lake in the world, there were two other flags that stood out to me. The first was placed on North Augusta, South Carolina, my hometown. I didn't need to read the name to know that it was put there by my mother. While some may find it odd that her favorite place on planet Earth is the town where she has lived her entire life, I think it makes perfect sense. To me it represents contentment, peace, and appreciation for what you have. The importance of those qualities instilled in me by my mom has been magnified throughout this month of meditation.

The second flag that stood out to me was pinned just under the top frame of this print of the world, not on any specific place at all. My initial thought was that it had been placed there by a child, playfully in search of his next reprimand, or by someone who didn't quite understand the simple instructions given. Since it caught my attention, I took a closer look. In doctor-like half-print half-cursive, it simply read "Wherever I am —L.C." I immediately inquired with the author of this tiny misplaced flag to ask if he understood the point of this exercise. Standing there on Patriots Point with the reception music playing in the background, looking out over the rising tide toward Sullivan's Island and Fort Sumter as the cargo ships came in, he said to me: "Why wish I was anywhere else? My favorite place is wherever I am. Right here, right now."

As my eyes welled up with tears, I felt the impact of his response and had the realization that he actually displayed the deepest understanding. I gave him a quick hug, hoping he wouldn't catch me becoming emotional. I was able to let out a quick response, "Thanks, Dad."

For me, this story reflects what I've been able to get out of implementing meditation into my daily routine. Presence. Appreciation. Mindfulness. Clarity. Simplicity.

Beware of the tail of the comet

John Steinbeck wrote in his book *Travels With Charley* of an epic road trip across the country with his dog in the late 1950s. This book was gifted to me by my parents on recommendation from a friend before my similar experience of travelling across America, nearly three quarters of a century later. Wanting to be sure I was the one stroking the brush on my own blank canvas, I decided to hold off reading Steinbeck and Charley's adventures upon my return. There seemed to be insufficient time to tackle the entire book before my departure, and something just did not feel right about reading a book about someone else travelling across America. . . while actively travelling across America myself.

There were many similarities and plenty of differences alike. Although difficult to refrain from comparison, my aim was to enjoy their story and experiences objectively, independent of my own. At some future moment, there will likely be a formally written account of my time on the open road, a product propagated from personal experience solely through my lens. Regardless, I thoroughly enjoyed Steinbeck's book, and either through time, location, or reflection, there were many pieces that stuck with me.

One of those pieces was in regard to presence. He could stop along his travels and use pay phones to make calls back to his life in New York. He described the effect of those calls like the tail of a comet: The engagement he experienced was never over when he hung up the phone. It was more like a descending trail of thought over a period of time. No matter the news or content of the phone call, it affected his ability to be fully present wherever he was on the road. Happy news, sad news, no news, just talk—all left a seed of thought in his mind that demanded attention for a period of time before he was able to return to the moment.

Think about that in relation to our present-day, distraction-laden existence. Long before the dominant use of cell phones and social media, Steinbeck found distraction notable and significant enough to write about in his book, impacting his ability to focus on what he was actually experiencing—and he didn't even call home every day. As noted previously in this book, we pick up our phones nearly a hundred fifty times per day! Holy shit, just think about that for a second. How are we ever able to be present?

Being aware that this is happening to us is certainly part of the battle. Awareness and acknowledgment are integral in meditation and mindfulness. When we identify a thought or distraction, and allow it to freely pass through without clinging onto it, the tail of the comet metaphor may disappear. Or at a minimum, the tail shortens. This is a practice, and not always an easy one. It might not look like a dramatic change overnight, but more of a subtle shift in perspective over time. With a growing level of awareness, we are able to better draw our focus to the present moment. A residual benefit of this mind state is that when we slow our thoughts and calm our minds, we become better equipped to address incongruence in our lives. We are able to address the root causes, rather than erratically put out fires all day every day.

We have access to more distractions today than ever before, so we must be vigilant in our commitment to care for our overall health and well-being. To further belabor the point of device and digital addiction, let's get back into it, this time in specific regard to presence. It's a serious and complex problem, as we are more connected to each other than ever before, yet we are more lonely, depressed, and stressed. The tail of the comet is overwhelmingly and exhaustively true in the form of social media. There is access by minors, fake news, silos created by an algorithm, and a laundry list of other issues. But the piece I would like to tease out here is simply, or perhaps not simply, the constant distraction. Every text we receive, every notification that pops up on our screen, every phone call we feel like we have got to answer right this second takes us somewhere else. The effect goes well beyond trying to remember what on earth we were doing seven and a half seconds ago.

In our brain, dopamine is released, which provides pleasure, motivation, and satisfaction. Serotonin levels decrease, which affects mood, sleep, and digestion. As a stress response, norepinephrine is released. This affects arousal, mood, and learning memory. All of these neurological responses in device addiction are similar to substance addictions. I recently saw a meme that said: "Before you judge an addict, put your phone down for 24 hours. Every time you think about it, that's what it feels like." It feels like that because, to our brain, it is that.

This repeated craving of stimulus, or addiction, has a major impact on the nervous system. Our nervous system is the "command center" of the body. This system elicits the behavioral reactions of fight, flight, freeze, or fawn. A healthy nervous system is able to move between these states when needed and return to a regulated state. When dysregulated, we are in active self-protection. We find ourselves in a stress response all the time without the ability to return to a baseline of regulation. When stressed, we often turn to negative coping mechanisms: binging, self-medicating, isolation, burnout. Sustainable behavior change becomes difficult, perhaps impossible, when we live in dysregulation. The chain reaction of negative effects reaches so far beyond the actual consumption.

The good news is that there are positive and healthy coping tools and strategies that promote sustainable behavior change. Mindful movements such as yoga, tai chi, and walking help to calm our nervous systems. Breathwork, cooking, creativity, dancing, singing, reading, music, art, and play are also tools that help with regulation. Repeated intentional experiences raise our awareness and cultivate presence.

Nervous system, presence, and mindful movement guru Nicole Griffin is a wonderful resource for further exploration on these topics. She offers coaching programs, online resources, and mindful international travel retreats that guide finding and leaning into your growth zone in a healthy, positive, and sustainable way.

It would be interesting to know how Steinbeck and Charley implemented coping mechanisms to draw them back into the here and now as they journeyed throughout the country. One way Steinbeck was able to experience his trip mindfully was through the eyes of Charley. He spoke often of Charley's interactions with great detail of sensory responses. It felt like it gave him purpose, perhaps even permission, to literally stop and smell the flowers. Being able to connect with our current environment by using our senses can be helpful.

The 5-4-3-2-1 method is a sensory grounding exercise that is used to reduce anxiety and stress. Please feel compelled to jump in and go through this exercise with me now. It is quite simple, and helps bring you directly to the here and now.

First, identify five things that you can see. Survey your surroundings, allow yourself to notice things you may not typically notice. What stands out to you?

Next, identify four things that you can touch. Notice their texture. They could be rigid or soft. They could be parts of your own body. Maybe something cool or warm.

Now, three things that you can hear. It could be your own breath. Is there a rustle of the wind blowing through the trees? If you are indoors, is there a low, steady humming of the AC or furnace? Perhaps there are children playing outside, a dog barking, cars passing. What do you hear?

See if you can identify two things that you smell. Food cooking, a perfume or cologne, or a nearby fire. If you are enjoying a coffee, acknowledge its smell.

Finally, identify one thing that you can taste. What is the most recent thing you have eaten or drunk? Can you still find the flavor on your taste buds? Maybe you recently brushed your teeth or are chewing gum.

Tools similar to this exercise were deployed quite often on my VanAm tour of the country. It was a real challenge to practice being present on the road. There was certainly the tail of the comet. It was a wonderful enhancement to be able to have buddy chats while driving hours of long, straight, endless interstate. At the end of many of those conversations—that held their own level of depth and weight—I would arrive at a destination with the expectation to be fully engaged and present. Often I would be arriving at a park or natural landscape for a trail run or hike. That type of activity breeds internal dialogue, thought, and reflection, but I wanted it to develop organically. I wanted to be able to enjoy interactions with other park-goers rather than be mulling over something I can't do anything about, something that was happening two thousand miles away. Again, not a bad thing to have to manage. . . but a thing to be managed.

This method helped to slowly integrate into whatever destination I reached. To be honest, my first sensory experience was typically the smell of a pit toilet at a park after hours of driving. Nothing will snap you into the here and now like the stench of one of those things. So, that part, not slow at all.

Outside of that repeated memorable experience, the sensory exercises were extremely helpful. I would step out of the van and stretch a bit and walk around my immediate perimeter, just to get the lay of the land. If it was a national park, I would go into the welcome station and grab a map, exchange pleasantries with the rangers and other tourists before heading back out to the van to plan, pack, and grab a snack. When packing or snacking, I would do so with the sliding door open, or with the windows down. Sights, sounds, and smells would always help bring me into the moment.

A second interesting dynamic of balancing presence on the road was the fact that I was living in a van.

When you're at home, you might experience this to some degree: You have some control over your morning routine, you get out of bed, get in the shower, fix coffee, and so on. It's your habitat and you are typically comfortable there. Then, when you walk out the front door into the world, anything can happen. Typically, your sidewalk is there, and your driveway. You take a similar route to work or to drop kids off at school.

It's different when you're traveling in a van. The inside of the van always looked the same, other than the amount of laundry on the floor at a given time. The picture outside the van, however, was ever-changing. On days when I drove into the night and arrived at a parking spot in darkness, I had no idea what I would see when I opened the door the next morning. I literally awoke next to mountains, and I awoke next to mole hills. (Well, OK, they were prairie dog hills, but. . . as the saying goes.) Every day was its own adventure, and it took great intention and presence to experience each as its own. Each experience at each place stood on its own merit, and I worked extremely hard to honor that.

Nikki joining for two weeks was a welcome addition for many reasons, and a nice test of my ability to be present. She shared updates of people and places from back home, and there were more phone calls. Not a bad thing, but while driving to pick her up at the Las Vegas airport, I did wonder to what degree I would be able to let go and simply be in that environment with her. I began feeling quite anxious.

Out of thin air, I suddenly created this expectation that I was responsible for giving her the best trip ever on her abbreviated two-week stint. Foolish to think I could control so many external factors. Also foolish to undervalue, and initially underdeliver, simply being together. That was enough for her, and I was interrupting that by trying to find the best campsite, most breathtaking views, and most challenging trails. It needed to be perfect. I created this unrealistic expectation of myself that became a void in the one area Nikki cared about most: spending intentional time together. Presence.

It was foolish, because she can rough it better than I can! She was the one talking me out of a frantic spiral a year earlier when I broke the heater in a van we rented in New Mexico on a night in the low twenties. I insisted that we drive thirty miles to a hotel in the nearest town at two in the morning. She was bundled up and sleeping. It was only out of my own insecurities and fear of inferiority that created this anxiety and tension. It was disconnecting from this moment in search of some perfect future moment. When that's the approach, it often remains the approach, even into the future. So, the result is that the perfect future moment never arrives. And the cost is double, because we end up robbing ourselves of both.

Then there was the social media aspect while out on the open road. Oddly enough, I was taking the master's class on addiction during the second half of the trip when I gave a presentation on digital and device dependence. There is plenty more to tease out in regard to presence. I wanted people back home to have the opportunity to follow along as much or as little as they felt led. Many people asked prior to my departure how they would be able to live vicariously through me, to show support and have a second-hand experience of what many believed to be a wild idea to embark on. To try to get ahead of the draw to this looming battle, I put together a loose plan before leaving for how I intended to engage with social media.

I turned it into a little bit of a game, where I would shoot a bunch of short videos of places I was visiting, down time at campsites, and other interesting things I came across. Then, at night, I would compile a video and do a voiceover describing the day, place, or event. My thought was I would have fun exercising my creative side, be able to share part of my journey with others, and, most importantly, not be consumed by opening social media apps once every six minutes. I thought I was executing my plan pretty well, balancing presence and engagement in the actual things I was doing with connection, and sharing with those in various other places. That is, until I got my iPhone usage report one Sunday morning to the tune of over eight hours per day. Um, excuse me, Siri, what?! I thought at first the "8" was a "3," and wasn't entirely thrilled at that number. Turns out, it was two and a half times that.

To be fair, I was using Maps quite a bit when navigating my route, and each night I did research for the next day, which ate up considerable screen time. And then there was the time spent creating my compilation video from the day that I had already justified before even pulling out of the driveway on day one.

Is that fair? This is what makes social media tricky. I had so much fun creating those videos, and I loved getting comments from friends and family, but did it stop there? Was it a healthy amount? Was I sitting by the Emerald Pools in Zion National Park, enjoying an apple, listening to the birds, watching the falling mist from cliffs above, or was I missing the serenity of an undervalued part of the park because it wasn't the highly sought after Narrows or Angels Landing? Was I shoving food in my mouth, reading comments about my previous day in Arches National Park? Was I comparing views from one video to the next, and was that impacting my living, breathing, actual real experience in those amazing places? At times, admittedly, sadly, yes, without question.

There are levels to this

A photographer spends weeks in Grand Teton National Park with aspirations of shooting the Lower Gros Ventre gray wolf pack. She has researched their movement patterns and current weather conditions, knows how many members there are in the pack, and how many of them are pups. She has immersed herself in their world, understanding how they operate, and acts in full reverence and respect of their environment. Days pass without seeing a single wolf, or bull moose, or grizzly bear.

Still, the photographer waits. She takes time to appreciate the surrounding scenery. The rocky Gros Ventre River comes into view moments after the first rays of sunshine illuminate the east faces of the Teton Range. A baby moose with his mama takes a swig of water to begin their day. The line of melting snow creeps farther out of the valley and up the mountains, welcoming yet another spring. The season of life, awakening, growth, and warmth.

This experience is many things for the photographer: joy, work, play, sacrifice, and purpose. Whether she gets the perfect shot of the gray wolves or not, she is immersed, content, and alive. There is profound meaning in her days and nights taking residence in the park. Of course there are challenges and difficult moments for her. Being present does not mean everything is all hunky dory all the time. It means we are aware of our surroundings, tapped into our senses, and connected to the moment we currently inhabit.

After many days in the Tetons, when the Gros Ventre gray wolf pack, including two pups, moves playfully across the grass just outside of the treeline, the photographer is in position and ready. She feels a tear run down her cheek as she captures this magical moment. One day her photographs will be published in a magazine. Soon, she will load a couple of her favorite shots onto her social media page, attempting to convey the magnitude of her elation in the caption.

But none of that crosses her mind at this moment. She is connected. She feels like she is, at least for a little while, a part of their world, and they a part of hers. Presence.

The photographer is so deep in the moment that she did not realize a van was pulling up adjacent to her off of a nearby access road. Before the van quite reaches a full stop, the side door slides open and six people hop out hastily with their cell phones at the ready. Full of excitement and conversation, the vanners snap dozens of pics of the same scene of gray wolves playing in the meadow. Some as selfies, some together, and others with just the wolves against the backdrop of the three Teton peaks. What a cool moment for them to experience together, knowing they were not likely to see several wolves out in the open like this.

As fast as they arrived, they are gone. A quick half-stretch and some chatter about the next wild animal sighting they can scratch off their list. They go on to see dozens of bison and elk, some pronghorn, and even a mama black bear with her cub before they descend back down to their Airbnb on the outskirts of Jackson Hole.

Their pictures, too, will soon appear on social media. Captions will also tell of their amazing experience in the wild. Close encounters with elk, selfies with wolves, hikes to waterfalls, and a peaceful lunch shared with friends along the bank of the serene Snake River.

One is not more right or wrong than the other. My goal is not to criticize the vanners; in fact, I want to celebrate them. They planned a trip to see something beautiful, engaged in intentional time with friends and likely now have stories to tell for years. When they return home, they get to go back to their job, family, or school and talk about something that they actually did. Something that pushed their boundaries, something they are proud of. Pushing ourselves outside of our comfort zone looks different for each individual person. It is not a competition.

The two stories above certainly show levels of engagement, and they offer varying degrees of becoming involved in something, and how it can be a progression. But when we engage further and deeper, we are more likely to create an environment that cultivates presence.

The immersive experience of the photographer, for me, illustrates cultivating presence. Having that level of depth in an experience is difficult to snap in and out of; it must be curated. I have been a vanner far more often in my life than I have been the photographer. These two examples help remind me, when in a park, natural environment, or even daily interactions, the value of fully immersing.

Are you taking a picture for some future social media reaction you may receive? What small steps can you make to deepen your connection in a given situation? Did you film the entire concert, or put your phone in your pocket, close your eyes, and feel the music? Are you driving to the top of the mountain for the view, or, if able, are you hiking the trail to reach the summit?

Some years back, two friends and I took a trip to Peru to hike the Inca Trail. We planned the trip rather hastily, impulsively, with the aid of a few beers over a holiday outing. This type of behavior is right up my alley, but I was still surprised it was actually coming together seamlessly over the course of one meal. One friend, Taylor, was living in Brazil at the time and was home for a couple of weeks during the holidays, so there were travel and logistical challenges with him. The other, Worm, had never been outside of the country. He had already applied for a passport for his upcoming honeymoon, but had to expedite it in order to accommodate our trip to the Andes. Within a week, flights were booked, our guide was secured, and we were immediately two months out from our pilgrimage to Machu Picchu.

Worm and I travelled together from South Carolina to Cusco, Peru, to begin our acclimation period, and Taylor joined a day later. We explored the city, ate at a local market, met with our guide Freddie, picked up any last-minute items, and were ready for the four-day trek through the Andes. Hiking the Inca Trail requires a guide and porters, who joined us from a small town near the beginning of the trail, and we were also joined in our group by a badass mother-daughter duo from Canada.

The most hiking I had really done prior to this trip was a few miles up and back to a waterfall or a local mountain summit. Living in the Southeast, the highest option is Mount Mitchell in North Carolina, standing just under seven thousand feet in altitude, and I hadn't even hiked it. I had been above fourteen thousand feet a couple of times in Bolivia prior to this trip, but mostly just walking around in communities, no real physical exertion at altitude.

And that was just me. Taylor had experienced some altitude sickness once before in Colorado, and Worm had not experienced any, but only because he had never been above five thousand feet. So, there were many unknowns for the Inca Trail, starting around nine thousand feet, and maxing out near fourteen thousand on day two at Dead Woman's Pass—the only stop on the map written in English, which is such a cruel joke.

Day one was fairly easy, and of course there was adrenaline and excitement for getting this journey under way. The three of us were sharing two tents, so we had worked out a nice rotation so we each had the opportunity to enjoy a solo night's rest in the peace of the Andean night. Our porters carried a dining tent, all of the cooking gear, as well as some of our belongings. They were all badasses, hauling dang near one hundred pounds apiece at a faster rate than we were walking with our measly day bag, and doing it in what appeared to be fifteen-year-old Chacos.

Into the second day, we had increased mileage and much more elevation gain. It started to feel like work. We also began coming across some of the Incan ruins. The beauty of this trek is hard to describe. Each direction at nearly every point of the trail offered a new, awe-inspiring view. Freddie, our guide, told us, if you see something you like, take the pic right then because the weather will change instantaneously. He was right. It would go from perfect sun and blue sky to sideways rain in a heartbeat.

By the afternoon of the second day, as we were approaching Dead Woman's Pass, we were living above the clouds, watching them calmly pass below us, and maneuver flawlessly around lower peaks. We celebrated at the top of the Pass with a shot of Pisco that I sneakily purchased and carried with me in my day bag for this exact moment. The difficulty kicked up another notch on the third day. We now had two full nights of sleeping on the ground and not sitting on a cushion, or anything else comfortable since leaving our Airbnb in Cusco. Soreness was creeping into my unprepared muscles and joints. It was a welcome discomfort though, falling deeper and deeper into the natural elements.

On days two and three, we came upon several massive Incan ruin sites that we basically had to ourselves. Hardly anyone was around, just us, a few other guided hikers, and my imagination. I was imagining to the best of my ability what it might have been like living in these dwellings a mind-numbing five hundred years earlier.

We walked the handmade, ancient stone steps, bathed in the streams, and slept on the ground. Of course we had more amenities, better first aid, guidance, and porters. We had our meals prepared for us. But to the level allowed by local laws and regulations, we dove in. I visualized what it might have been like, studied the history, and listened to the guide and locals we passed on the trail. It was an incredible experience.

On the fourth and final day of the hike, we started earlier than any other day. We awoke around 2 am and made our final push. Nearing the end of the hike, completely exhausted from the compounding soreness, stairs, hills, peaks, valleys, and fatigue of the previous three days, we arrived at a set of extremely steep stone stairs. It took hands and feet to scramble up to the top, at which point you walk through the Sun Gate to end the Incan pilgrimage, and for the first time, lay eyes on one of the most breathtaking, spectacular sights that man has ever created: Machu Picchu.

Our guide Freddie gathered our group of five for a hug, a mini-celebration of our achievement, and a photograph with the ancient Incan city below us in the distance. The Sun Gate is certainly a photo op location—other guided groups were arriving nearby at the same time. People were walking up from the site to take a pic from this incredible vantage point. Those folks rode a train from Cusco to the nearby city of Aguas Calientes, and took a bus up a steep, winding road that landed them at the front door of Machu Picchu.

Again, this is not to say those bus riders did not experience something amazing. I am sure that they did, and they have a story to tell and pictures to show that 99% of the world does not have. Meanwhile, when they show the exact same picture that I show, I have a different story to tell. There are levels to this. I am not making assumptions whether those tourists felt more or less present than I did.

When we engage in an activity, a trip, or time with a loved one, there are opportunities for deeper immersion. Whatever level of engagement we end up in, are we fully there? Are the bus riders wishing they were me while at the Sun Gate, or are we sharing a beautiful moment in the here and now? As I was scrambling up the rocks to the Sun Gate, was I worried about things to do back home when we finished, or was I breathing in and out, and taking it all in? Was I present?

PART II

ADVANCE

Allow Yourself to Feel Emotions

Searching for relief

Author's note: This chapter treads into some heavy content around mental health, depression, and suicidal ideation. If these topics are a trigger for you, I suggest that you might want to skip this chapter. If you are currently feeling and experiencing thoughts of suicide, please know that someone cares. I care.

Once upon a time, as mentioned briefly in the section on Engagement, I began seeing a therapist. Like many people I have come across in my life, I had zero interest in taking part in this exercise. It was dumb, they didn't care about me, my problems were bigger and different than everyone else's, they would never understand, and on and on and on. I wish I had a count of the conversations I've had with people over the years who have shown resistance to seeing a therapist. The reasons, or excuses, are way too many to list. There are many who, like younger me, believe their problems have passed the point of help. So broken that it can't be fixed. The "I'm sure what they do works for some people, but there is no way a shrink will be able to offer me anything useful" people. Many of us also use resistance to therapy to justify nothing being wrong with us. "Thank God I don't have a 'problem' like so and so has." Let me clue you in. We all have problems. It's a part of the human condition. It is my opinion that anyone could find benefit in a process that allows you to better understand yourself, how you feel, why you feel that way, and how to make sense of it all.

There is no finger wagging at any of those who have previously, or are currently, resisting therapy. I get it. I have been firmly in that position. There were many times it was suggested to me, and I took serious offense, and shunned the thought. I mentioned earlier how engaging in therapy changed the trajectory of my life, and in this chapter we are going to dig deeper into how I began to see myself differently through the counseling process.

What initially led me to my first encounter with a therapist was a failing relationship, or so I thought. At least that is what got me in the door. My girlfriend at the time and I were hanging on by a thread to a situation we both knew was comfortably past its glory days. Both middle children, we struggled to cut the cord and move on. Both emotional, both had some "woe is me"—hers much less than mine—and both people pleasers, who felt a level of obligation to be there for the other. It is, of course, because we cared deeply for one another, and it was a recipe for a messy, never-ending cycle of shared misery.

My failing relationship received all of the blame for my emotional and mental health struggles at the time, but it was much deeper than that. I got my college degree like I was "supposed" to do and began working for a great company. It was a good job, and I was very fortunate, but early on I felt like I did not fit in. Being the low man on the totem pole, I felt an overwhelming pressure to show up as the version of myself I thought they wanted to see. It seemed like I had to put in extra hours to keep up with others, and it was exhausting. Frustrated and burned out, I would come home each afternoon and drink. There is a strong drinking culture in, well, everywhere it seems, but certainly in the environments I found myself throughout my career in industrial sales. So it did not seem wrong, bad, or out of the ordinary to come home and tie one on. Hangovers began impacting my performance at work, which led me to drink more.

This growing feeling of worthlessness, sadness, and frustration began disrupting my relationships with family. There were fewer calls to mom and dad, and eventually fewer trips down the one-hour stretch of I-20 that separated us. I still showed up for holidays and birthdays, but with far less engagement, and zero presence. I knew that I was not representing my family in a positive way, which made me feel even more worthless, and I saw myself as a disappointment.

I was always somewhere else mentally, and had begun drinking at a considerably higher volume. If I did not drink around my family, I was thinking about it; and leaving early so that I could go and do just that.

With the encouraging atmosphere within my industry, I was able to fly under the radar as far as performance, attendance, and employment were concerned. Maybe that was helpful to pay the stack of bills on my kitchen table, but I also used that culture to justify my behavior. And, if I'm honest with myself, I probably didn't know how much it was actually affecting me.

The combination of drinking, isolation, and trying to hide my misery all led to a financial situation. In my late twenties, although I was receiving positive feedback from managers, and had even gotten a couple of promotions, I was not exactly bringing home the bacon. I purchased my house at one of the worst times in history, 2007. There was no real reason I should have bought a house at that point in my life anyway, and I was quickly upside down. Fortunately, a few friends of mine lived with me to help cover the mortgage. But I was still drinking all of the time, and depressed, and I was trying to hide the fact that I was upside down on my house with increasing debt, so I went out and partied on an irregular basis.

The failing relationship finally led to some level of closure, although I did not view it as helpful at the time. She got engaged. I found out on Instagram of all places. This was the early days of Instagram, and I just started my account, so I didn't really know what was going on. I tried to talk myself out of believing it. It was a close-up picture of her left hand holding a wine glass, with a new, shiny ring on her finger. The caption read, "still celebrating." With the benefit of hindsight, it is pretty obvious what was going on there.

As I said, I blamed all of my negative behaviors, thoughts, and emotions on her and the relationship, but the reality was it was a culmination of all of these things. They all fed off of each other, and I came to realize that they all boiled down to one thing: me dressing up as someone else, because, for whatever reason, I was not enough as myself. I was not good enough for a girl, so I had to buy a boat and a motorcycle. I was not good enough for my job, so I put a mask on every single day, dressing how I was supposed to, saying what I was supposed to, and leaving *me* at home. I drank and partied and acted a fool around people because there was no way anyone actually wanted to hang out with just *me*. Hell, I didn't want to hang out with just me.

There was a downward spiral unfolding right in front of my eyes, and in many ways, without me really noticing, or certainly without me doing anything about it. Of course, I knew I was not happy, but I did not realize the speed at which my life was tanking. Mentally, physically, emotionally, spiritually, financially, you name it.

All of these contributing factors had me in a really rough spot. To the point that I decided I was going to take my own life. Thankfully I never made an attempt, and as a result I am here today. Far too many others are not as fortunate as I am. The suicidal thoughts overwhelmed me and consumed every aspect of my life. I could not sleep, I could not work effectively, and I failed to carry out normal daily tasks like laundry, paying bills, hygiene, and nutrition. It seemed like all I could do each day was drink, avoid, and smoke weed to cope.

My soon-to-be-engaged ex-girlfriend encouraged me to try seeing a therapist. She actually called several places for me, searching for a good fit. Each place told her that they were appreciative of her caring and reaching out, but that if I was serious about going to counseling, then I would need to set up the appointment myself. So, mostly in an attempt to prolong our situationship, I booked myself an appointment to see a therapist.

Between the booking of the session and the actual session is when she got engaged, which sort of changed my tune on the entire ordeal. I was ready to scrap the whole thing and keep on digging my hole of unhappiness deeper and deeper. It was a great talent of mine to suppress everything I was feeling and put on a mask in front of everyone else. But after the engagement-seen-on-Instagram, I felt a larger sense of panic than ever before. I had already been having suicidal thoughts and ideas for some time by then, and she was the only person with whom I felt that I could share my emotions. I certainly didn't always tell her the severity of which I felt those emotions, and how seriously I was contemplating taking my own life, but if I ever felt like I was about to burst, I could at least tell her something. That would grant me some form of temporary relief.

Finding others who accept your emotions

It's crazy how certain people come into your life at just the right moment. I had a roommate, Jenna, at the time, who had moved to the city where I lived to pursue a graduate degree. We had actually grown up in the same neighborhood and attended the same church as children, but didn't know each other very well at that time, as she was a bit younger than me. We became fast friends once reconnected, as if we had been besties since kindergarten.

So when the Instagagement happened, Jenna was there to pick up the pieces. We lived together, so she was more informed than most, and knew everything wasn't hunky-dory in my life, but much of it came as a shock to her as well. As soon as I told her about the engagement and that I needed to talk to her, she leapt into support mode. I unloaded onto her everything that had been going on in my world behind closed doors, and more importantly, in my mind. That day we rode around in my car for what felt like three days and five minutes all at the same time. I cried, she held space. When I eventually was able to get out actual words that resembled English, she listened.

For years I had jumped in my car alone when I felt overwhelmed. Almost always after drinking heavily and with thoughts of worthlessness and despair. As I said, I never made an attempt to take my own life, but I continuously put myself in reckless, dangerous situations. I would think that I didn't want to be selfish by directly taking my own life, but if I damaged my body for long enough, or got into a car accident, that it would take care of itself. Sometimes I drove alone for hours, with no agenda and no idea where I was going. I drove interstates, and I drove rural back roads. I would end up in places where I had no idea how to get home, and I didn't care. For this, and many, many other reasons, it is a miracle that I am alive.

I recently wrote a song on my guitar about those nights. Here's an excerpt of the lyrics:

'Bout halfway to Charlotte, with an ending in my mind
and the ending ain't the city, I won't make it there alive

Can't tell if these pine trees are blurred from the beers or
from the speed,

the depth of my pain growing deeper each shallow breath
I breathe.

The ringing in my head, should I be answering the call?
One day I'm gonna do it, and there'll be no pain at all

I close my eyes, and drift away

Forget what I have to say

I close my eyes, tilt my head back

Set the cruise and relax

I close my eyes.

Those car rides changed after the day Jenna and I rode around. That setting would become an outlet where I felt a sort of permission to share with her, cry, yell, whatever the situation called for. It became a fairly regular occurrence for us to cruise around the city together. Of course I didn't want to put her in danger, so I was in a different state of mind when she joined. At a minimum, I was far less intoxicated, which was a decent start. It was like she had a Spidey sense for when I needed to escape. We could be at the house, out with friends, or at a sporting event with thousands of people, and every single time I needed it, she was ready to roll, no questions asked.

Kind of funny: One night we actually got pulled over as we were looping several times through a neighborhood. I'm not sure if someone called in our suspiciousness or if the officer happened to be there at the same time as us. I had been crying, I think Jenna had also shed a tear on this particular night, and we quickly tried to get it together as the cop approached the driver's side window where I was sitting. He asked why we had been driving laps in this neighborhood, and I told him we were just driving and talking. Noticing the scratch in my voice and tears on my cheeks, he abruptly realized he certainly must have stumbled upon a breakup or something of the sort. He quickly, and apologetically, let us know people get suspicious when the same car rides up and down a street. He asked if we could handle this elsewhere, tipped his cap with what felt like an understanding compassion, and let us be. In hindsight I can't help but wonder if he, too, was struggling mightily with something, and also used that method in an attempt to sort it out. We never really know what people are going through.

There is no way to adequately articulate how vital my friendship with Jenna was during that time. When I told her I was not going to keep the therapy appointment, she adamantly protested. She told me I didn't have to go forever, but I should go once. She drove me to the first session to show her support and nonjudgment and told me, "I don't care what y'all talk about, but I'm going to watch you walk in the door, sit in the lobby for an hour, and watch you walk out." I walked in and out of my therapist's office every Tuesday at 11 am for ten years.

Jenna also drove me to our hometown and dropped me off at my parents' house to tell them that I had been thinking about taking my own life. It was something that needed to happen for a long time, but I always managed to talk myself out of it. I'm not sure I would have ever had that conversation had it not been for her. Similar to therapy, she dropped me off, left me for a while, and came back to pick me up when I was ready. I honestly don't remember the ride back that day. I'm not sure if we talked, cried, or sat in silence. Maybe a combination of all of those, but whatever it was, I am one hundred percent sure that it was exactly what I needed.

A short time later, we sat together and worked up an email to send to a select few of my friends to let them know what was going on. This is something I had gone to the most extreme of lengths to avoid for years, and with Jenna's support, we made it happen. I made the first pass on my own, with the understanding that she could proofread it before I hit send. Apparently I minimized the severity of the situation significantly. There were several jokes in there, mostly at my own expense. That was a defense mechanism. I didn't want to ruffle any feathers or inconvenience anyone else and their wonderful life with my bullshit. Jenna convinced me that they all cared, and I would want to know if any of them were going through a similar situation. We sent the email. Each of them reached out to me individually in their own way.

The very day I unloaded all of this on Jenna, she was set to go out of town to shop for her wedding dress. A monumental day in her own life, she made sure I was in decent shape before taking off. Without me knowing, she reached out to our friend Heather to see if she could come hang out with me in her absence. Heather spent the entire day with me, and sat at my house until I fell asleep. She also asked no questions, and never once acted as if she had been inconvenienced. There were many other times she showed up in service to me. So many people have since played a significant role in helping me through difficult times, most without ever knowing to what depth.

There was still an uphill battle to be fought, and plenty of work would come, but after going to my first therapy appointment, visiting my parents, and sending the email, I felt a mountainous weight lifted from my shoulders. Yes, I was involved, and it is important to acknowledge our own role in healing, *and* none of this would have happened without Jenna. So, Jenna, I'm eternally grateful for you and the role you have played in my life. I would not be here if not for you.

Awareness and tools for self expression

When talking about feeling emotions, prior to this I had never allowed myself to feel anything. All of my responses to anything that had the slightest odor of emotion were to effectively numb, avoid, and cope. Yes, I cried often, like, really often, but I never sat in it. It never crossed my mind to allow myself to explore why I might be crying, that there may even be some value to expressing my emotions in this way. I viewed it as wrong, weak, and foolish. I certainly didn't let anyone know that I was crying every day, typically multiple times per day.

When I first started seeing my therapist, Kim, I did not feel comfortable sharing my emotions with her either. I went to the first appointment out of some fabricated obligation to Jenna only to justify not being there on my own volition. But I went. Eventually, some of it started to sink in. If nothing else I was forcing myself to sit in it, even if it was only for one hour a week. I was certain I was doing therapy wrong, and nothing positive was coming of it. She would ask questions and make observations, and I would talk. Many times early on, my talking consisted of letting her know how she didn't, and most likely never would, understand what my situation was like. It was a lot of rambling on and on. So often I felt like I was talking in circles—which I probably was—and getting nowhere—which I probably was not.

Even when I thought Kim could never understand where I was coming from, she never passed any judgment. She was an objective listening party who allowed me the space to be as I was. I began feeling differently when I left her office. My comfort level with the environment incrementally grew each passing week. It became a place where I could just emote. I got angry, very angry, many times, at myself and others, and Kim just listened. She didn't tell me that I was wrong or that I should not feel that way, but rather she validated my feelings. She allowed me to cry without jumping in and telling me everything would be OK. She didn't show discomfort or anxiety, or urge me to stop. Her creating this space allowed me, possibly for the first time, to simply feel my emotions. I always had big emotions; I just never knew it was OK to have them. I tried, and successfully by some measures, to sweep them under the rug.

I still was not prepared to share, or even acknowledge, these emotions out in the real world for quite some time. It started with one hour per week in Kim's office. Then it started to bleed over into my ride home; sometimes I sat in the parking lot of her office for an extra hour just crying. But then I would smile. I began taking this idea home with me and, behind closed doors, became more and more comfortable with the fact that I am an emotional man.

I could never have admitted that before. I spent so much time and energy trying not to get emotional in front of people, that I was literally missing my own life. There have been dozens of opportunities to speak at friends' and family members' weddings, celebrations, and funerals, each time coming up with an excuse of why I was not able. I was terrified to cry. I was terrified that others might see me cry.

So, how do you begin allowing yourself to feel your own emotions? First, you must develop self-awareness. My antennae were extremely sensitive to others' actions and behaviors, but I had no awareness of how I actually felt about anything. People would talk about high-tension topics, such as politics and religion, and I had no stance. I just agreed with whomever I was in the presence of at that moment. With a certain group of friends I might feel one way, and then at a work event the same day I could feel the complete opposite. This probably applied to low-tension topics too. It was worse than apathy: it was fraudulent. The reason it never felt wrong is because I had never taken the time to discover my own views on anything. This is a dangerous place to be. Vulnerability is difficult, which we will talk about shortly, but you become vulnerable in this state as well. You become impressionable, manipulatable, and easy to take advantage of.

In your job, are you answering questions and acting based on the way you feel deep down, or the way that will make you the most money, satisfy your boss or investors, or get you the most engagement on social media? Do you know how you actually feel about the topic? Do we even ask ourselves these questions? Are you showing up as a different version of yourself in different environments? I don't mean that in a flexible way, I mean are you compromising values, morals, beliefs? Have you identified your values, morals, beliefs,. . . and feelings?

When a particular emotion comes up, do you suppress it? Do you make yourself busy rather than acknowledge it? Do specific emotions or situations make you feel uncomfortable? Might I suggest leaning into that discomfort and explore it further. You may be able to identify patterns that have developed.

It could be useful to speak how you feel out loud. I know this sounds woo-woo, but give it a shot in a closed room while you're by yourself. Examples are:

"Every time X calls, I feel a flutter in my chest."

"It makes me sad to lay down in my bed alone."

"It pisses me off that I cry when I think about X."

"I get this weird feeling of excitement every time I run into X around town."

Practicing mindfulness can also be helpful. Although it has become culturally cliché in the United States to say we should be more mindful, true mindfulness practice can deepen presence, awareness, and engagement. Mindful breathing and breathing meditations are great tools to bring us to the here and now and heighten our awareness.

Jon Kabat-Zinn is widely regarded as someone who exposed the Western world to mindfulness. His book *Wherever You Go There You Are* was incredibly helpful for me when first discovering the topic. It helped inform my perspective on how I exist within the world around me, and in short, my awareness. I began to understand that my response to things happening around me were not the same as my feelings about those things. Once able to separate the two, we become less driven by external factors, and more driven by awareness and essence.

Journaling and reflecting also help to show us what we notice throughout a day or given period of time, and our feelings toward our interactions. While I was on VanAm, I adopted a journaling practice from my time in corporate America, oddly enough. When I was in sales, each week I was to submit my weekly notes. The way that we approached this was to summarize important takeaways that take fifteen minutes to write, and five minutes to read. We called it the 15/5. It makes sense to me because it is enough to capture the things that really matter, while still short enough to where it doesn't feel like a huge task to complete. So, each morning I woke up in the van, and before I got out of bed, I reflected on the previous day for fifteen minutes. This model can be applied to creating a habit of identifying and expressing emotions.

When learning to feel our emotions, it is important to understand that we are not only talking about crying, sadness, and gooey feeling stuff. It is also about how to accept happiness, excitement, and appreciation. The full range of emotions exist to work in harmony with each other. They arise because your body is telling you something. When given attention and acceptance, the emotions lessen in intensity once they feel satisfied. It is when they are ignored that they are exacerbated. So, when something makes you happy, it is OK to be happy.

This reminds me of a passage written by Thich Nhat Hanh, a spiritual leader, teacher, and often called "the father of mindfulness": "In us there is a river of feelings, in which every drop of water is a different feeling, and each feeling relies on all the others for its existence. To observe it, we just sit on the bank of the river and identify each feeling as it surfaces, flows by, and disappears."

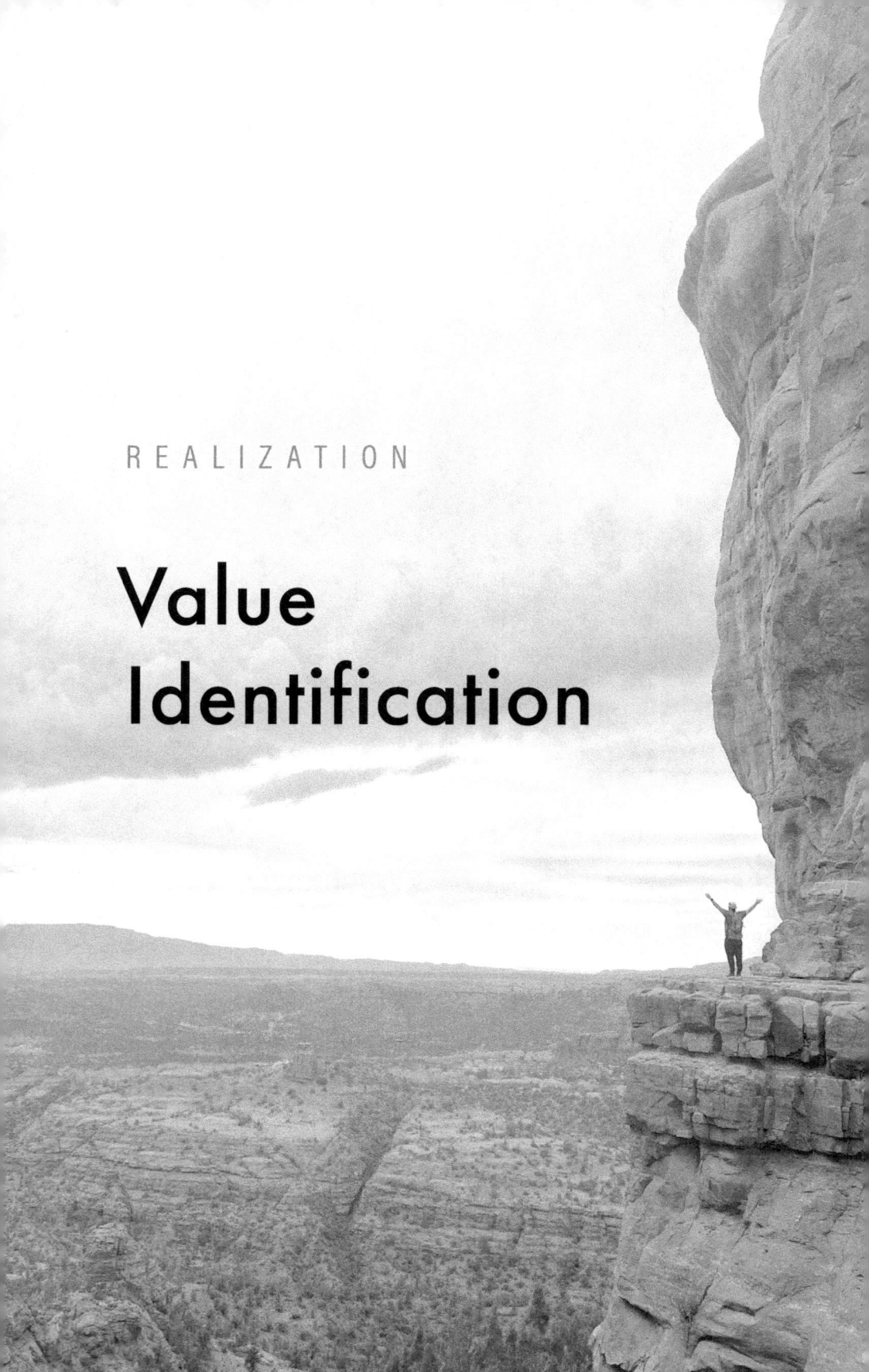

REALIZATION

Value
Identification

The 'Big V' and the 'Little V'

Learning to feel and accept our emotions as they arise is about acknowledging what is already within us. In the example of my life, I am an emotional man. That is the way I was wired. Once I was able to accept that, it became one of my greatest strengths. With a raised awareness, identifying emotions in the moment helps to address them and manage them before they fester. Suppressed emotions never die, and always have a tendency to reappear bigger and badder than ever.

Once able to feel emotions purely and honestly, the pressure we previously placed on ourselves begins to dissipate. As goes the ask in the Serenity Prayer, "grant me the serenity to accept the things I cannot change." I find a certain freedom in that—a weight lifted, one less thing I need to be consumed with. What that freedom allows is more space in our mind and body to think and feel authentically. It creates the space for us to address challenges with a clearer mind, and expand our capacity for potential growth.

Once we allow ourselves to feel emotions, it can become more apparent what is most important to you in life. This sounds obvious, but the better you know yourself, the better you become at pursuing meaning and purpose. One way to go about this pursuit is through identifying your values. Value identification is about recognizing and verbalizing the things that we hold in the highest regard.

We are going to talk about openness to change next, so not to get too deep down that road now, but this does not mean once you identify your values they are set for life. Identifying values is a process of reflection, realization, and understanding to be used to inform decisions and behaviors. It can be fluid over your lifespan. It might be helpful first to talk about what values are, and how they fit in the decision-making process.

There are levels within values. Many things in your life can hold varying degrees of value, worth, or meaning. There is a difference in things that can hold value and in your main, core values. It might be helpful to look at them in the categories of "big V" values, and "little v" values.

Little v values are things that do hold importance, that you might enjoy and prioritize, but if you lost them it wouldn't feel like your identity was completely compromised. These are things that you value. Like for me, having a cup of coffee on a cold morning. That enriches my life, especially if I am doing it with Nikki. It makes me happy; it holds value. But if our schedules changed or we ran out of coffee one morning (which would never happen in her house), it would not change the fabric of who I am. I value playing the guitar. I am extremely passionate about playing the guitar, and it is something that adds an incredible amount of joy to my life. It holds value. These are little v values.

Big V values, however, are often regarded as core values. These are about what means the most in your life; it is central to what you care about. I hope no one reading this dies on a hill, but when thinking of what hills you might be willing to die on, it could be due to one of your core values. What is the most important thing in your life? What do you believe in? What do you stand for? What do you refuse to compromise above all else? The answer to these questions should either be, or be driven by, your values.

If you have never done a values exercise, well, no time like the present. There are lists of values (integrity, family, simplicity, etc.) that you can find with a quick internet search as a starting point. Having a comprehensive list in front of you can be helpful as you begin to think through your own personal values. It becomes difficult for many of us, because so many of the value words sound great. You might resonate with over half of them. That is wonderful.

Now, try really hard to narrow your list down to your top three to four core values. This might take some time, because it is difficult to feel like you are "throwing away" so many great words. Don't worry. It doesn't mean if you throw away "honesty" that you are suddenly dishonest. You can still be honest, just as you were before looking at this list. This exercise is more about the words that you do choose.

As you whittle the list down to a handful or more, a different perspective might help. Think about how you would react if someone said you did not appear to value the word at all. Go through your remaining words one by one. Your initial reaction, the feeling in your body of resistance when saying certain words, might help you get your list to a top three.

Reminder: Once you have landed on three, it does not mean you are tied to them forever, or that you cannot change. Look at it more as a guide, as a system of checks and balances. I view them as a filter in decision making. You can now run the decisions in your life through the filter of your values. What does that mean? I will use myself as an example.

The three values I have identified as my nonnegotiables are family, achievement, and authenticity. So let's say I am applying for a new job, or even a new role within my current company. When I review the description of the new job, the skill set needed, the time and travel requirements, and the purpose of the new job, I look at each of my core values individually.

First, I think: *What would my family think about this job? Would I be able to spend adequate time with my partner, kids, parents, etc.? Will my being in this role improve the lives of the people in my life that mean the most?*

If I were to take this enticing new role, would I be able to achieve something meaningful? As achievement is one of my values, I can tell the difference when I go to bed at night if I feel like I achieved something meaningful or not. I am a completely different person. Meaningful achievement is specific to the person, and you must determine what each of these values means to you. For me, I am driven by feeling like I have made an impact on someone else's life. I also thrive off of feedback affirming an impact has been made. That is how I landed on achievement.

Lastly: *If I take this amazing role that is being offered to me, will I be able to show up as myself every day?* Remember earlier, when I shared about having major depression and suicidal ideation? That was directly related to my feeling like I could not be myself across several domains of my life: social, relationships, work. I was inauthentic, and it almost cost me my life.

So, if the answer to any of the questions asked in the previous three paragraphs is "no," then the decision is made for you. It makes the decision-making process much easier, because if you have to compromise any of your core values, then you can confidently and clearly know that saying "yes" would not serve you and your best interests.

An alternate (or fourth) core value for me would be connection. I thrive off of relationships with others. Oddly, when I'm exhausted, I can actually recharge my battery by being around other people. If I were offered a job where I would spend 90% of my time alone in an office or cubicle with no human interaction, that'd be a no-brainer "no" for me.

Oftentimes we take jobs, or make certain decisions, based on what society tells us, or what the next person thinks, or simply how much money it will bring us. We also make decisions to please others, not rock the boat, and suck it up. If none of those things are in alignment with who we are as a person and what we believe in the most, why are we making decisions based off of them? That is why I love the values exercise: it offers confidence in decision making, and it makes it so much easier to say no to the things that aren't in your best interest.

I also like to think about this in terms of time allocation. Now that you have identified your values, you know what is most important to you in your life. Now, think about what you spend the most of your time doing. If they don't directly serve your values, there is a misalignment. You might feel stuck, frustrated, and pooped all the time. Because you are spinning your wheels and pouring energy into places that you don't ultimately care about. When there is a congruence between your values and your time allocation, there will likely also be more contentment, fulfillment, and peace in your days.

Examples of identifying values

In this chapter we will look at some examples of identifying values. Again, yours will likely differ from the examples here, but it could be useful to walk through the process of determining what you value, and why it's of significant importance.

Reflection is a large part of this process. It is one thing to identify our values, and it can feel phenomenal to articulate a more defined realization of what we stand for at our core. Once these values have been identified, though, a periodic evaluation, or check-in, is healthy, when you can ask yourself: *Are my values still aligned with my actions?* There are likely areas of alignment *and* opportunities for re-engagement. Determine areas of improvement and allocate time appropriately. This is not a start from scratch, and really not even a "correction." It's more of an active and flexible role you are taking in your life in the present moment.

Are the core values that I have selected still of the utmost importance to me? It is OK to change and select something that most speaks to you at this moment in time. Consistency tends to be something we celebrate carte blanche, but it is not always quite the badge of honor we portray. Yes, consistently shooting free throws will likely make you a better free throw shooter. Consistent reps in booking public speaking gigs will undoubtedly make me a better public speaker. Consistency is critical for growth.

Yet there are also times when consistency is touted as a positive when it feels to me like fear, excuses, and a lack of growth. If my voting record is the exact same for sixty years, have I been open to new and different ideas? Maybe, maybe not. Have I actually listened to anything that wasn't what I already believed or wanted to hear? It takes courage to give an honest reflection, and allow permission to be honest with our present circumstance and situation. We must allow for growth, evolution, and change; both in ourselves and others.

As shared previously, a large part of my Advance in Solitude is dedicated to reflection—in all areas of my life, and part of it is certainly in regard to my values. For instance: *Have I prioritized my family over the past year? Are the achievements I have listed over the course of the year meaningful to me and my overall mission? Am I aiming to achieve things for the sake of recognition, or am I working hard on things I care about in an effort to make a positive impact on the world around me?* (If so, the achievement should be a byproduct.) And most importantly: *When I reflect on the past year, have I shown up in every environment as my true, authentic self?*

This whole process might look different for you, but allow yourself the space to reflect. When intentional, incongruences in values and behaviors tend to jump off the page. At least for me they do. And when they do, it immediately informs my goal setting and process building. I will share a couple of practical applications from my own life in hopes they help create momentum in your doing the same.

A couple of years ago at the Advance, I kept getting stuck on the values piece. Actually, I kept getting stuck on the core value that I mention first each time I say them out loud: Family. When reflecting on the previous year, I didn't feel like I had put forth adequate energy in this area. I saw my family a good bit, talked to them with some frequency. Compared with others, I probably logged more hours communicating with my family than the majority of people I know. But I am not interested in making that comparison. I did not feel good about it. Life gets busy, and it had gotten busy for me. Other areas of interest dominated my time; growth and expansion were happening elsewhere, and I was incredibly proud of the payoff from the work I put in. None of it was a bad thing. I didn't do anything wrong. I simply noticed an inconsistency in my values and how I allocated my time. I got caught up.

Thanks to this annual check-in, I was able to identify this incongruence, and immediately put a plan in place to help recalibrate the way I was spending my time. As I meditated, hiked, ran, and reflected over a few days in the mountains, I pondered creative ways that I could have more meaningful interactions with my family.

I had been thinking about how wonderful it was when my parents, my two siblings, and I were able to get together in the same place. I mean, for fifteen years we all lived together in the same house, and we were all we had. Day in, day out. Sporting events, church, holidays, summer break, and every day in between, it was just us. Always outside, playing basketball, ping pong, or any other sport. Or in our playroom watching Scooby-Doo, Fraggle Rock, ThunderCats, and Saved by the Bell. We literally had a piece of furniture in our house that I would have sworn was manufactured, marketed, and sold as "the Scooby-watching chair." That is all I have ever known it to be called.

Occasions spent with all five of us together look much different these days, and that is a wonderful thing, too. Our outings now include significant others and children, which allows for new relationships to be built and fostered. I began thinking about how fun those days are with the entire crowd, and realized there never feels like enough time for meaningful conversation with each individual member. Rightfully so, much of our energy in current family settings is poured into the young people. I cherish those moments with my nieces and nephews, and the togetherness of the collective. I also felt myself missing the one-on-one interactions of more depth.

Thinking through this at the Advance, I decided I would like to job shadow each of my parents and siblings at their current place of employment. We "spend time" regularly, but do I really know what any of them do on a daily basis? Do I know how they interact with the people they spend more time with than anyone else? When I talk to them on the phone, I would like to have a better idea of what is taking place in their lives. Of course, I want to know how the kids or grandkids are doing, and I definitely want to relive experiences and stories from the good ol' days. I want to recognize them for the human being they have grown to become today! I am certainly not the same person I was twenty (or even five) years ago. So, I committed to taking an interest in that same evolution and growth of the members of my original family that I shared living quarters with for fifteen years of my life.

In a recent episode of The Constant Quest Podcast, we had a guest talking with us about Human Design. I encourage you to look up your design, especially if you are into personality assessments and astrology. With only your birth date, time, and location, you receive an entire report based on I'Ching, chakras, and astrology. I am certainly not the expert, but our guest Natalie Neal Hassett is, especially through the lens of marketing and branding. She read over my design and offered possibilities of the way I might see the world. Some felt more or less accurate than others, and some felt right on the money.

The reason I bring this up is because one part of my design that stuck out to me was in direct connection with my values. Achievement. When I first learned about identifying my values, I had a tough time with all of them, but the toughest was achievement. I wanted to show that I am selfless and empathic through my values, not that I want to win. Yes, I have some competitiveness in me, but I also want to see my people win. I want humanity to win, society to win. But every time I thought of replacing "achievement" with a different word, something stopped me. I have never really been able to explain it, but it's different from just winning. It is different from making money, which is an achievement, but not one I care a great deal about. I have viewed it differently from accomplishment, because that can feel like simply checking a box. I don't want to complete something just for the sake of completing a task; that feels boring and not valuable. What I want to feel is fulfillment. I want to feel like I've done something meaningful, to me and the world. That is how I view achievement, and why it has remained as one of my core values.

While on our podcast, Hassett articulated perfectly how I have felt all of this time. She basically said, perhaps when you go to bed at night, you feel content and fulfilled from your day and you are pleased with the outcome, and subsequently sleep well—or you feel like today did not meet its potential, you have an unfinished or unfulfilled feeling about it, and you have trouble going to sleep. No in between.

She went on to say: Fulfillment might come from relationships, connections, and personal payoffs for work that you have put into something. YES. Yes, that is exactly how I feel. Achievement to me can be similar to the way I look at the word "successful." We get to define what that means to us. What I view as an achievement might be different from the next person, but it is incredibly important to me at the end of each day to feel like I have achieved something meaningful. My mere sleep, health, and regeneration is dependent on it! I would say that qualifies for a core value.

Previously I described my early personal struggle with depression and suicidal ideation. Without understanding and identifying my values, I had no direction and no vision. Every single area of my life was suffering because I felt, in each setting, like I had to show up as someone other than myself. I was inauthentic. The stress and pressure I placed on myself was constantly overwhelming and crippling, because I was trying to show up how I thought I was 'supposed to', or how others wanted me to. The people pleasing led me to develop a constant need for acceptance and positive feedback. Feedback can be incredibly valuable. I believe it to be core to growth and leadership.

Feedback can also be dangerous. I relied so heavily on feedback to the point where my expectations grew unrealistic. It is exhausting to pour all of your energy into trying to be perfect in everyone else's eyes—an impossible and fruitless task. When I did not get exceptional feedback, I would spiral. I began making up feedback. If someone else at work got praised for something that I was not even involved in, I would go home and mope because I was a terrible employee and no one liked me. It sounds ridiculous writing it out, but the most petty of things drove my depression deeper. All because I craved acceptance. I craved acceptance from others because I did not accept myself. I had no idea who I was, what I cared about, or what I stood for.

That cost of being inauthentic nearly ended my life by thirty years old. Fortunately for me, I stumbled my way onto a lifelong quest of self-discovery and self-acceptance. I worked tirelessly at learning about me. *What were my interests? What were my passions? What type of self-expression felt most genuine to me? Like if no one else were around, what did that look like for me?* Authenticity has become my key to success. No one is better at being you than you! It's ironic that, once I stopped obsessing over people's acceptance by trying to act how I thought I was supposed to act, and started showing up as myself in every environment, I learned that it's contagious. It is infectious. I get more unsolicited feedback about how inspiring it is to see someone show up as themselves. I never understood that before. So, because the absence of authenticity nearly ended my life, it should go without saying that authenticity is one of my core values.

Hopefully these examples of how to identify your values proved helpful. They should be different for each person. Explore what those nonnegotiables are for you. What makes you tick? Does the void of a value make you feel like it would compromise your ability to still be yourself? This exercise can be enjoyable and rewarding, as is anything that allows you to learn more about yourself. It can also be difficult, uncomfortable, and scary. It could very well bring resistance. That is normal. That is OK. Your willingness to meet discomfort head on is where the growth happens. Are you open to change?

REALIZATION

Be Open to Change

Navigating the stages of change

Seeing a counselor for more than a decade, and now being a counselor myself, have taught me that the crux of our growth lives in being open to change. That might be an obvious realization, and it's certainly easier said than done, but the importance of our own openness can't be overstated.

Some of the previous chapters in this book can help to encourage, or even unlock that openness. Exposure and engagement could open your eyes to a world otherwise unknown, to interests you didn't even know you had. Intentional time with self and others may be the impetus needed to get the wheels in motion. Presence and meditation may create the space for new and different ideas to enter without judgment, pressure, or expectation. Identifying our own emotions and becoming comfortable with who we are as an individual helps us to better realize the things that we are capable of changing, and prioritize what we actually want to be changed.

Part of being open to change is being open to new and different ideas, being open-minded about topics we previously held in a strict, one-sided view. When we understand it is OK to lean into and explore our emotions, we're more open to express them freely. When we identify what we stand for through our values, we can more easily engage in these new and different environments with more confidence. When our nonnegotiables are known, we get more clarity, and hopefully encouragement, to explore uncharted waters in other areas.

Empathy is critical. Can we look through someone else's lens, or at least attempt to do so, to better understand a vantage point never before considered? Being open to change takes vulnerability, and vulnerability is hard. When trying to open ourselves up to the possibility of change, we are almost always met with resistance—from society, family, institutions, history, and certainly most commonly from ourselves.

It's easy to confuse resistance as a warning sign that says, "Danger! Keep out!" Stepping out of your comfort zone, which I'll delve into more in a bit, looks different for everyone, even different for the same person across points of their lifespan. But, resistance itself is not a bad thing. Resistance is much more manageable when we focus on regulating our nervous system, welcoming the present moment, and understanding and accepting our own emotions.

Acceptance plays another major role in change. Drawing from the prior section on mindfulness, meditation, and presence, accepting that things are as they are in this moment can offer much-needed clarity on exactly what needs to be changed. Accepting something does not necessarily mean agreeing. It's common to hear comments like, "that is unacceptable" or "I am not accepting your apology." That can put us in a denial mindset, when we are not taking all current factors under consideration. Those comments often come when we don't agree with something. Acceptance is more closely tied to awareness and acknowledgment. Often, what we are not accepting is how we feel about the thing we cannot control, not the thing itself.

For example, I denied and resisted the fact that I am an emotional man for much of my life. I did not *accept* it to be true. It was easier, I thought, to pretend it wasn't the case, and tried to suppress it in hopes that it would go away, and under no circumstance was I ever to admit to anyone this weakness was part of my identity. It's still difficult to manage at times, and I still get emotional in moments I would probably rather not. The difference now is I have accepted it to be true. No longer am I lying to myself out of ignorance or denial that I have big emotions. Fuck it, it is what it is. I have accepted it to be true. Only at that point was I able to move forward with meaningful change. It can still be hard, but at least it is now possible.

In twelve-step programs, acceptance is on the list as the sixth step, but what is more interesting is that there is a heavy dose of acceptance required for the very first step: honesty. How often can we create and tell a false narrative to the point we actually end up believing it to be true? I'll answer for you: very often. Both meanings of the word are extremely important: Accepting things as they are, what do I know to be true in this very moment? And acceptance of self and others, which is my understanding of step six in the twelve-step model.

Acceptance can offer us the openness to receive things that might differ from how we know them to be, or want them to be. It allows us to be open to change. Change in mindset, change in belief system, change in behavior, all are possible with awareness and acceptance.

In psychology, there is a model called the stages of change. It is a conceptualization of the different points an individual experiences when trying to change a particular behavior. The five stages are pre-contemplation, contemplation, preparation, action, and maintenance. By name alone, these are fairly straightforward, but it might prove useful to walk through them in an example. This model can be applied to a change in any area, but here we will use substance use cessation, specifically alcohol.

Precontemplation, broken down in South Carolina slang, translates to "man, I ain't even thought about it yet." It might be in the form of denial, ignorance, or simply no desire to make a change. There is not even foresight in this stage to make an eventual future change. This may take form in the way of loved ones encouraging an individual to drink less, seek help, or even acknowledge damaging behavior due to drinking, and the individual not willing to accept the message. It could also look like an individual continuing to drink excessively in public with friends, struggling with relationships due to drinking, and drinking alone until they pass out. In this scenario there may not be a resistance to friends or a conscious denial, but a contentment in their current behavior and circumstance.

This would be a good place for a graphic showing how precontemplation exists in relation to the other stages of change. I view it as a big circle with the steps that actually embody change being inside the circle, and precontemplation being on the outside looking in. There is no movement yet, no momentum, and in short, no change. Perhaps it could be seen as a marker, or charting point, included only to show that the next step does, in fact, show movement. At a minimum, if all of the stages are written out, I believe precontemplation should be written in a slightly less visible font, to portray its rightful proximity to extinction from the list.

The largest difference between precontemplation and contemplation is movement. There is some form of activity, even if only in thought. There is still no accountability or commitment to change yet, but the wheels are turning. This is huge! When I talk about being open to change, it begins right here. It is easy for us to see someone who is ten years sober and crushing life and think, *I will never get there*, but at some point, they, too, were right here. This is the stage where many of the words we have been talking about enter the picture: awareness, feeling, acceptance. I'll also add curiosity, an extremely underrated quality to possess.

Each stage yields its own unique challenges, and contemplation is no different. Feelings of sadness and anger may begin to surface when realizing, *I drink wayyy too much*, or *my behavior when drinking is a danger to my family*, or simply, *man, I think I might have a problem*. It may also be difficult when thinking of the monumental task it will likely be to never drink again. The good news in this stage is that you don't have to *never* drink again—you are simply opening up to the possibility of change actually existing. I don't want to oversimplify the challenge this stage can present. People stay in this stage anywhere from a couple weeks up to a lifetime. Knowing and understanding the additional steps could be helpful for someone in contemplation. It may also be beneficial seeing and hearing others that have moved on to the next stage.

The third stage is preparation. Acceptance and awareness move more firmly into curiosity, possibility, and planning. This stage is also sometimes called determination. It moves the narrative of "I drink too much" to "I am going to do something about my drinking!" There is a commitment to action. This is a research- and gathering-of-information stage. The strain in this stage is that you are getting closer and closer to action. You are becoming aware that friendships could look different, the makeup of your social life could also look completely different, and previously "normal" environments can become uncomfortable. The flip side of this, with continued research and preparation, is that you realize you will save tons of money, along with some embarrassment and regret.

No matter what change we are talking about—it's not specific to substance use—there are positives and negatives. It's healthy to weigh both, and to filter them both through your values.

A healthy support system is critical in all stages, and it may begin to take shape during the preparation stage. Not one that reprimands, belittles, and finger-points, but one that is understanding and nonjudgmental, offers grace, and asks how they may be of service. Assembling and leaning into your support system is certainly part of the preparation.

Some relationships no longer serve the direction you are moving. That's OK. This is where you decide to separate yourself from those who are pulling you down, or who, at the least, are not accepting of your decision to change. Remember, acceptance does not mean agreement. My support system consisted of bartenders and friends who continued to drink, but they supported my mission. They held me accountable for what I was trying to achieve. I had bartender friends that would push another unknowing bartender out of the way and reprimand them, in support of me deciding to act in a way I felt best served me. Many of them went out of their way to make sure my water cup was full or that I was feeling OK in the environment.

By the way, I am explaining these stages as I have seen them from my own experience, not necessarily from a clinical perspective.

The preparation stage is often skipped in excitement and anticipation of action. There is no "always right" or "always wrong" way to approach this, but it is much more likely there will be regression if some level of preparation has not been applied. I see preparation as a foundation and base of knowledge that provides us with some confidence to move into the action stage.

You must determine for yourself the balance to strike between adequate preparation and action. Too little preparation runs the risk of unsustainable action, and too much preparation runs the risk of never reaching a point of action. Lean on your support network and trust your intuition. You cannot account for every single thing. At some point you need to give it a shot.

This moves us to the stage of action. At this point, you have become open to change. This is the payoff of your hard work. This is the actual day of the marathon. You have done all of the training, and of course it will still be difficult, but you are now built for this. The action stage is where you actually modify your behavior. You can also change your environments and experiences, but ultimately you are interrupting the cycle of a specific undesirable behavior.

The action phase requires resilience and grit. It is unfamiliar territory, and it feels uncomfortable. It is hard. Lean into the discomfort. It helps me to gamify it, to welcome it as a challenge. Each day stands on its own merit. A loss one day does not mean you have failed the mission. While the aim in this example is cessation, we could do a better job of how we measure success. Oftentimes we put so much pressure on ourselves thinking we have to quit drinking forever. I get a lump in my throat when I think I can never ever have another sip of alcohol again for the rest of my life. It might be coach speak, but I'm trying to go 1-0 today.

When you have worked so hard for something, and you do revert back, of course it feels like failure. It can be extremely deflating. My perspective though, is that it's only one day in the course of an overall picture. You are still in the action stage. Let's say you have gone two and a half weeks without drinking, and then you drink one day. You are 16-1. Damn, that's a helluva record in the NFL. That is a Super Bowl contender, probably even the favorite. The one loss is an obvious blemish, and it hurts, but it doesn't all of a sudden negate every other win. If the loss comes in the playoffs, maybe it stings worse. Maybe you got injured in the loss, maybe it was to your rival, maybe you even got in an altercation and got sidelined for a period of time. It all sounds terrible in the moment. . . but it's *one loss*. When the next game comes, put on your pads, lace up your cleats, and do everything in your power to make this one a *win*.

In the above stages of change model, there is the allowance for fluctuation between stages. It is common for people to regress from the action stage back to preparation, or even to contemplation. Without regression, the action stage lasts up to about six months. At this time, the undesired behavior has been altered, and a new behavior pattern has been created. This moves us into the final stage of the model, which is maintenance.

During maintenance, an individual continues to become more comfortable with their new habits and behaviors. They continue to gain and develop skills that support this new part of the identity. The support system becomes more solidified, and the new behavior becomes the status quo. Awareness is still critical, as are understanding what led to this stage, why it became necessary to change, and the progress that has been made in eliminating the undesired behavior.

Again, the example was specific to alcohol, but it can be applied to countless areas of your life. It is much easier and sustainable to stop texting an ex when we have recognized a desire to do so, identified why it is a positive change, and put together a plan and process to execute. Every time you want to text them, text your best friend instead, or walk a lap around the house, or play a particular song. Whatever works for you, do it. Just make it one day, then another. The feeling of a win becomes contagious.

Maybe you are miserable in your job. The stages of change can really be applied here as well. If you already know you hate it, you might already be in contemplation. *Are you open to change? What would that look like? How can you prepare?* Do an interest inventory: *What are things that you are passionate about? What are you good at? What can you make money doing?* Begin researching jobs in those areas. Prepare. Have a conversation with your partner. Build a support group. It might require sacrifice, like saving money, moving, or selling nonessential possessions. Push yourself to move into the next stage: action. Put in your notice. Determine a start date at a new employer. Open an LLC to start your own business. Act.

Whether it be behavioural change or situational change, time is an important factor to recognize. No question we get antsy for the change to have already become a reality the very second we recognize our desire. We also have to be realistic. Things take time. It definitely takes discipline, consistency, and patience to go through a cycle of change. But to return to the theme of this chapter, you must be open.

Fear is the other big bad wolf in this conversation. Nothing destroys our openness to do something more than fear. This is what makes change scary: it's unknown, and we don't like that. Fear arguably appears as early as the precontemplation stage, even if it is subconscious. It is also what makes the jump from preparation to action so difficult. Many people live in preparation for the rest of their life due to fear. It takes a great deal of courage to move through these stages, to take a chance in life, to make a change. It takes courage to become open to change. As author Joyce Meyer writes: "Courage is not the absence of fear. It is action in the presence of fear."

When circumstances suddenly change your plans

In 2018, I went on an international volunteer construction trip to Nicaragua. My mom and I were having lunch at Whiskey Kitchen when I received a text from my friend Bobby: "You want to go to Nicaragua next year?" *Well, yes, in fact, Bobby, I would love to. Where is Nicaragua again?* After very little back and forth, I was game. He was going with a group of people from his church, and someone had backed out after dues were paid and plans were set. That person agreed to fund the entire trip of the newbie if they could find someone at late notice to go in their stead. That newbie was me.

It was not an incredibly difficult decision for me to jump on board. I had been involved in five trips similar to this in years past, all of those to the country of Bolivia. My experiences there largely shaped my understanding of humanity, service, and gratitude. I briefly spoke previously of the feeling I had on those trips, one I have yearned to replicate since.

Each time I was in Bolivia I thought that I could see myself living there one day. Most of my time there was spent in and around a city called Copacabana, which sits on the shore of Lake Titicaca. I loved the culture, the people, the views, the simplistic way of life, and the appreciation. My visits only lasted for ten days at a time, but the impact was much larger. Upon returning home each time, I felt a strong tug to return to the people there.

Of course, Nicaragua is a whole other country, and different in so many ways from Bolivia, but there was a feeling of excitement over the similar structure of this upcoming adventure. I imagined many of the same factors that drew me to Bolivia would still be present. My curiosity can barely be contained in situations like this where everything is new and different. I am so interested in the ways in which others exist, believe, and feel. I am a people person, so I looked forward to the aspect of working alongside a bunch of strangers for a common goal. They were strangers from both the local community and within our group, as the only person I knew was Bobby.

In hindsight, another significant source of my excitement was vulnerability. Although I might be viewed as impulsive and spontaneous by those who know me, and I do acknowledge those to be true, an experience like this still exists outside of my comfort zone. I was with a group of people whom I viewed as having a genuine confidence in their Christian faith, while I was confused, conflicted, and interested in learning additional avenues of spirituality. There were also concerns about sleeping in a bunk bed in a room full of strangers, going the whole trip without drinking alcohol, and by some miracle, keeping my digestive tract in some state of normalcy.

Even in the face of all of that I went. . . and I loved it. I was open to change. We were in an extremely impoverished area of the country and worked alongside some of the most incredible people I have ever met in my life. Don't tell them they are poor—they will immediately tell you of everything they have in their life. Love, joy, family, community, and hope. As soon as the project started, I instantly felt connected. Connected to the land, the people, and that feeling I had longed to feel again. It was a beautiful landscape as well, with lush fruit trees everywhere around us. When we walked around the area, a local would grab fruit from random trees. I saw and tasted fruits I had never even heard of, and they were freshly harvested right in front of my eyes.

On our last day there, we were all asked to come stand in the front of the building we had been assisting with for the past ten days. The emotion of the moment overwhelmed me. I sat in it, I felt it through my bones and in my soul. I feel it right this second as I write these words. It is difficult to describe, but unmistakable when felt. Tears poured from my eyes, down my cheeks, and onto the floor. I closed my eyes. . . and I smiled. I allowed myself to feel every ounce of emotion in my being, unlike I had been able to throughout the entirety of my life up until that very second. I didn't care who was looking, what someone might think of me. I did not feel weak, broken, or exposed. I felt whole.

Unapologetically, I looked to my friend Bobby standing beside me as I was hideously smile-crying, and he was doing the same. Without words, we acknowledged each other with a nod, and shared the depth of the moment, together. Engagement, intentional time with others, presence, and feeling raw emotions, all culminating in an experience neither of us will soon forget. One of our new young friends behind Bobby appeared to be taken aback by our teary expression, possibly in part because we were men. I turned to her and said, *"que, esta lloviendo aqui."* The three of us shared a laugh, and she gave me a big hug, suddenly unbothered by the fact that "it's raining in here."

Diego, who hosted us, was walking across the front of the building thanking us for our contribution of time, camaraderie, and labor. As he walked up to me, with a calm, understanding grin, he hugged me and said, "I have stood right where you are standing, and felt what you feel. I will see you again."

After being back in the States for a few weeks, I could not shake the overwhelming connection I felt to that place. Yes, it was a good connection, but attached to that feeling was a forceful pull impossible to ignore. I listened. While pulling into my driveway in South Carolina one day after work, I phoned my boss at the time, and told him I was moving to Nicaragua.

Maybe it was impulsive, maybe it was emotional, or maybe it was an openness to change. Prior to that, I had been too afraid to change anything. I just lived the status quo, woke up everyday, did basically the same thing, and was unhappy with the outcome. My therapist, Kim, and I had been talking for probably over a year about my inability to make a change, even in the midst of my discomfort and displeasure. We talked about possibly moving into a different house in the same city while keeping the same job. Or staying in the same house and finding a new job. We even talked about staying in the same house and just asking my manager if there was another role within the same company that made sense for me to transition into. I was unable to do any of them. I was too afraid of change. And here I was decidedly moving to another country, alone.

My boss was the first phone call that I made. I figured if I called him first and quit my job that I would actually have to move due to loss of income. I was convinced. My parents resisted, offering voices of reason, safety, and legitimate concern. Many friends questioned my motives, reasoning, and sanity. I did not care. I have a hard time making decisions in general, and it was uncharacteristic of me to be this sure.

To further confirm my certainty, I did what any rational, sensible person would do. I reached out to three people who I knew would give me the answers that I wanted. The first of the three, my brother, is the same person I call first to discuss any other significant question in my life. He has travelled a great deal, and a heavy concentration of that travel has been to Central and South America. He is also partly responsible for getting me into travel and cultural exploration as he, my sister, and I went on a monthlong backpacking trip across Europe my senior year of college.

The other two people I contacted were both living abroad at the time, so I knew they'd be on board. My friend Donald, who grew up in my neighborhood, was living in Africa with his wife and two kids. The other, Taylor, was living in Brazil at the time after moving there from the states on an assignment with a US-based healthcare company.

Although I felt confident these three would be in full support and encouragement of my decision to move abruptly to another country, they also were folks who I knew had invaluable insights, recommendations, and advice in this particular area. They each offered up many things I had not yet considered.

The wheels were in motion. There can be a beauty in the unknown: potential, possibility, creativity. A blank canvas awaited me, and I was at peace. I felt a trust in something much larger than me that everything was going to be OK. I was feeling more in touch with who I was as a person through counseling and leaning into my emotions and desires. I had confidence and understanding of my own morals and values, providing a guiding light as I entered into the depth and darkness of the unknown. I was free. No longer bound by self-imposed pressures to do right by everyone else, live up to some unrealistic expectation, or fall victim to the ever-present fear that had been driving my life for as long as I could remember. Finally, I was open to change.

Change became constant in my daily life over the ensuing few months. My employer and I came up with a timeline of three months for the date of my departure. The people in my district had been great to me over the past decade and a half, so I wanted to be helpful where I could. The job search for my replacement began, and I would stay on and help with training and their transition into my role. Each day I dutifully worked on small projects preparing my house to go up for sale. I sold possessions on Marketplace, donated other items of value, and delivered truck loads of stuff to File 13.

Diego, who became my primary point of contact, began communicating regularly. He and his organization agreed to house me for a period of time until I got on my feet and found my own place. In exchange, I would volunteer with their programming and help out where I could. He helped tremendously with Visa and other logistical questions, reassuring me that everything would be a proper clusterfuck and work out just fine. I had him searching for a nice (read: functioning) dirt bike to be procured before my arrival so I could easily move about the area.

Two months out from my decided departure date, I bought a one-way plane ticket from Atlanta, Georgia, to Managua, Nicaragua. By then I was mentally checked out. I was hanging by a thread to stay motivated and helpful at work, and friend conversations and interactions became dominated by my upcoming move. Mentally I was tasting the fruit, visualizing my new life. I was swinging on a hammock in a tank top and bucket hat without a care in the world.

A couple of weeks prior to my flight, I got a call from Diego. In summary, he expressed his excitement over my willingness and courage to take such a leap, *but* there was some news he had to report. Things had drastically changed. Some political tension came to a head with widespread violence surfacing throughout the country. He told me that, with the current socio-political climate, and inability to safely travel the roads from Managua, there was no way that I could make the trip anytime soon.

(I have a hard time making this all about me, because the situation in Nicaragua was dire for millions of people. Keeping within the context of this book, however, I am going to stick to the impact on my impending move.)

My initial reaction was to panic. *What was I going to do now? Should I still just go? I don't have a job! How am I going to make any money? Where am I going to live? What am I going to tell everyone?* These were the immediate thoughts and questions that entered my mind. I was facing decades of conditioned beliefs of worthlessness, inadequacy, and brokenness. I felt myself reverting back, losing hope, and getting angry. But all of the work of the previous sections of this book was not for nothing. This time, I sat in it, acknowledging and accepting all of the feelings expressing themselves through my mind and body. I was able to gain some clarity on how to handle this news. I refused to return back to the same life I had before, knowing there was more.

What a great test and opportunity this was to see if I had really become open to change. I called a friend to see if I could stay in his and his wife's spare bedroom for a while, and they immediately said yes. I called the director of operations within my district at work and told him the news. Before I could even ask, he said: "Don't worry about it. You've got a spot here." An entire new job was created within the district that did not exist before, just to allow me to continue to work there. I was grateful for the gesture by many people in my organization to make this possible, and it was also validating that I was viewed as an asset. I'm not sure if I was ever told that before, and if I had, I never heard it. That new role led to another role, which was better suited for my skill set. I was taking better care of myself than ever before *and* performing better at work. I was making considerably more money than I ever had. Family and friends supported me emotionally, when they easily could have pointed out all of the reasons I shouldn't have wanted to go in the first place.

I never boarded the plane to Nicaragua, but everything had changed. I knew for the first time in my life that if something did not work out, everything was going to be OK. My mindset had changed. This was only possible because I had been putting in the work for years to prepare myself for this moment. Yes, I was scared. Yes, there were significant risks. And yes, it went completely differently than what I had prepared for, and it all worked out. I am so much better off because I was open to taking the leap.

This looks different for every person. But change is essential, even helpful. For example, if you are depressed, and you continue to sit at the same desk, sleep in the same bed in the same house, drive the same car, then all of those things become associated with the depression. Something has got to give. It might be a change in employment, a change in geography, a change in relationship, or a change in mindset. It does not have to be something seemingly gigantic as my option of moving out of the country. Start small, and watch the dominoes fall.

It would be five years after Nicaragua when I actually left my company, but the changes were happening, one encouraging the next: changes in behavior, a change of mindset, and preparation for what was to come next. The passion to be of service to others was the throughline in all of the experiences that led me to that undeniable feeling I mentioned previously. I began applying to master's programs in the mental health field, and selected a counseling and rehabilitation program. I went to school at night for two years while still working for the same employer before hanging it up for good to embark on a brand new journey.

Learn to Appreciate Impermanence

Redefining failure

We have so far looked at two angles of being open to change: the openness to create change in our own lives, and how we handle and manage changes that are out of our control. Another way that I have come to say this is to learn to appreciate impermanence. This speaks directly to our ability to be present, and take a role of engagement in our own lives. Right here, right now, because things don't last forever. We talked about this in the Spend Intentional Time Alone section, in regard to not putting maximum effort into things that no longer serve us, just because we have always done them. Now that we have more of a foundation, we will explore this further.

The idea of impermanence was heavy on my mind throughout my VanAm trip across America. Just before leaving to go on the trip, I had been talking quite a bit about impermanence with Taylor, my friend and cohost of The Constant Quest Podcast. We talked about how it's OK for things to serve us only for a while, and when that time is up, we don't have to regard it as a failure. With that perspective we can view it as a positive. Not so much that we need to hold onto the things that once served us, as a way to cling to past good experiences before they disappear. Moreso that there lies an exciting potential of what might serve us in this new moment. It can change, it can be different, and that is OK. We don't have to justify it to anyone else, and we do not have to be embarrassed that things changed and that we are now going in a new direction. We place a lesser value on things that we think will always be there. Understanding impermanence has helped me to embrace presence and hold this fleeting moment in a higher regard.

Within this context, we need to redefine failure—or, at a minimum, refine our perspective on failure. I love hearing professional athletes, coaches, and high achievers say that failure is a necessary component of success. Failure can be a wonderful teacher, motivator, and spark to get moving in a desired direction. I will take it a step further and ask: Are the things that we consider to be failures actually failures at all?

A friend and I once started an outdoor and adventure company called Good Vibe Junkies. We had some pretty good ideas, some cool logos and designs, and renewed energy and excitement in our lives due to embarking on something amazing. Starting the business inspired us to take trips together, and in general, spend more intentional quality time together. We were rapidly learning new skills and having more in-depth conversations, rather than venting frustrations over corporate America, which had plagued many of our prior interactions.

We had so much fun. I won't speak for him, but I viewed the whole experience as extremely valuable. Successful? I guess it depends on your definition of success. Going through the steps laid out in this book, I have come to understand that I get to determine my own definitions of success and failure. Our company never blew up, and we did not make much money to speak of, but were there no successes? Was it a failure? Do we classify it as a failure because it had a shelf life, a period of time that served us, that eventually came to a close?

It created experiences I wouldn't have otherwise had. I learned an extraordinary amount of things, by engaging in something I had no idea about. We created an LLC, which I had never done, talked with graphic designers, screen printers, apparel companies, and outdoor retail stores. I began researching branding and marketing, because there was an immediate interest at hand. Part of our model was to shoot videos of our adventures and travel as part of our brand identity. So, I learned how to edit video and audio. I researched platforms, formatting and editing tips, and social media strategy. I wouldn't know about any of that stuff if not for Good Vibe Junkies, and it did not cost me a dime. Is that not a success?

There were a few people that supported me in that venture, but the vast majority of feedback I received was negative in nature. *Why did it fail? I knew that wouldn't work! It was crazy to think that was going to be successful. What did you learn from the failure?* Learn something, yes, a lot of things. Failure? I'm not so sure I categorize it that way.

Even if we do call it failure, why is that looked upon so negatively? It makes me think of the Michael Jordan commercial from years ago where he says, "I missed more than nine thousand shots in my career. I've lost almost three hundred games. Twenty-six times I've been trusted to take the game-winning shot, and missed. I have failed over, and over, and over again in my life. And that. . . is why I succeed." This is coming from the greatest basketball player of all time.

I believe triumph, at least in part, could be defined as the endurance of defeats. Failure becomes part of success. Why, then, do we view them as opposites? Of course, we must learn something from the defeats, and use them as a teacher. But too often we feel like we need to categorize something as a success or a failure, as a way to see how we stack up against others. The way you define success could be completely different from the very people you are trying to compare yourself to. Zoom out: there is a bigger picture.

There is value in analytics and evaluation, and I'm not suggesting to scrap them by any means. Still analyze, reflect, and learn; all of these breed improvement. What I am saying is that if you fail at one thing, you are not a failure; actually, you are taking a necessary step toward success. And speaking of impermanence, the failure is also temporary, so weigh it accordingly.

Are you resisting a healthy impermanence by a fear of change? A fear of failure? *I don't want to run this business anymore, but I have run it for twenty years. What would I do if not for this business? I can make it work, I will not fail. I'm going to sell this product this way because that's how my mother or father did it.*

What if that product is now obsolete with a changing world, or a new and better product is available? You know what would be a bigger failure than shutting the business down in many cases? Never shutting the business down, or refusing to adapt and change with the times. I don't want to oversimplify it. I understand there are many nuances to situations like this, and they do take deliberation, time, and reflection. I also know that there are many of you reading this who know they are in a business or a role at work that has well since passed its value to you. Are you open to change?

I field questions and statements all the time regarding my decision to leave my perceived stable, great job, and there are probably ten times more comments that I haven't heard. I had a lucrative role within a company full of people whom I really enjoy being around. I developed some incredibly meaningful relationships through my work there. The company had the highest market share in each of our regions—and by a large margin in my specific area—and the division I worked for showed healthy growth each year. The position I most recently held fed into many of my strengths, I had flexibility, and I had developed quite a few deep relationships with clients, vendors, and co-workers. This sounds amazing, right? Why would I leave?

Some components were certainly amazing, all of the things I just mentioned plus more. Now I get to walk away with those amazing memories and experiences intact. I am able to see it for what it was, appreciate all of the many ways it shaped who I have become as a professional and a person, *and* recognize I am now better served pursuing other opportunities.

The bottom line is it should not bother us when people question our decisions to make a change in our lives, but it's worth talking about because many of us struggle with it. I know I do. For years I would have a wild idea and get up the courage to mention it to someone, and the very second they shot it down, I would scrap it and categorize it as a bad idea. This contributed to my depression and low self-worth. It exposed my inauthenticity by allowing another human to dictate what was, or wasn't, right for me in my life. Far too often, the people whose approval and agreement we seek to gain are not even living the type of life that speaks directly to us!

It might be valuable to flip that around and view it from the inverse. I spent too many years of my life wanting to be accepted by others, wanting to fit in. The more I explored my emotions, allowed myself to dream, and identified my values, the more clarity I gained around who I wanted to be. I began to realize I had different interests from the people I wanted to fit in with, as well as different beliefs and different goals. Each time

I've stepped out of my comfort zone and followed a passion, dream, or crazy idea just for me, the outcome has been incredible. With that data, I started to think it was more of a positive to have ideas no one else had, to see things differently, and to trust and follow the internal whispers—and eventually screams—to pursue what brings me joy. So, now if I do happen to share a crazy idea with someone, I become more amped up, excited, and validated when they do *not* seem to think it is a great idea. Because remember: Not all crazy ideas are great, but *all* great ideas are crazy.

Trust yourself when you know something has run its course. When there is an undeniable fire burning inside of you, do you deny it? Or do you accept the impermanent nature of life and growth, and pursue it relentlessly?

Unwavering stillness in the ebbs and flows of life

When it comes to appreciating impermanence, there can be beauty and simplicity in knowing that we don't have to make all of the decisions. Instead of resisting, perhaps we practice acceptance and presence. It brings to me a high appreciation for the things that surround my everyday life, functioning just as they are meant to, with or without me. The ebbs and flows, the ups and downs, the seasons, life and death. It is all ever changing, and through that impermanence, I feel connected.

Jon Kabat-Zinn speaks directly to this feeling in *Wherever You Go There You Are* as he describes the mountain meditation. An excerpt of his passage here:

> *Now, as well you know, throughout the day as the sun travels the sky, the mountain just sits. Light and shadow and colors are changing virtually moment to moment in the mountain's adamantine stillness. Even the untrained eye can see changes by the hour. . . As the light changes, as night follows day and day night, the mountain just sits, simply being itself. [...] Calmness abiding all change.*

Kabat-Zinn goes on to describe the changes through the seasons. Each brings its own conditions and characteristics to those looking on, but all remains the same to the mountain. We have the ability to show up as the mountain, solid and still, as the world moves around us. We are a part of the process, *and* we can sit without reaction.

Life is full of ebbs and flows. We live and we die. Nature grows, falls, and replenishes. We are surrounded by impermanence, in the days we live and in the relationships we hold dear. Finding solace, peace, and acceptance in the cycle of life brings presence, and increases the value of our days. Impermanence is a certainty, embrace it.

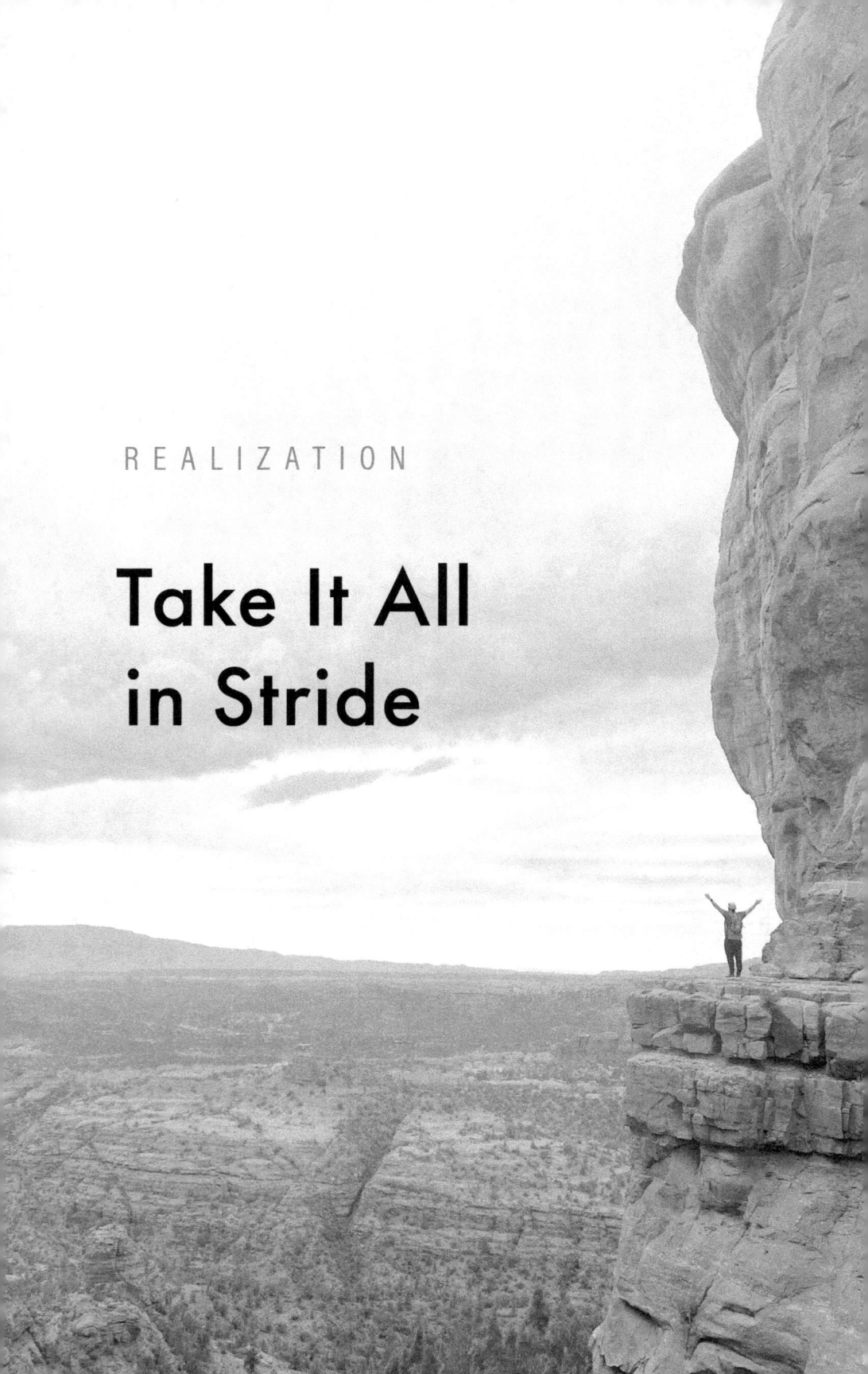

REALIZATION

Take It All in Stride

Get comfortable being embarrassed

While on my VanAm road trip across America, I was fortunate to be joined by Nikki for two and a half weeks. My trip from east to west had been highlighted by four friend visits, culminating in my driving from Zion National Park to Las Vegas one evening to pick Nikki up from the airport. I had certainly been in some cities—Nashville, St. Louis, Kansas City, and Denver—but the overwhelming majority of my miles would best be classified as rural. I leaned into the rural elements: the vastness of the landscape; the slow, simple, quietness of the towns; and the space available within which to operate my vehicle. This is not to make any excuse for the upcoming story, but let's just say I was not adequately prepared to navigate the city of Las Vegas.

My goal was to cut it pretty close to Nikki's arrival, and Apple Maps suggested an easy, stress-free, two-hour poke through the desert. It was a lovely drive, and difficult to imagine a city would soon pop up along the route—which is exactly what Vegas does. It's kind of amazing. I kept saying out loud, "Who decided to put a city here?" It felt so out of place, plopped right inside a natural landscape. Regardless, it was a welcome sight because I was excited to see Nikki and experience the next portion of the trip with her. The ride ended up being smooth sailing over from Zion. Until I approached the airport.

I was complimenting myself on my expert efficiency, as Nikki's flight was scheduled to land about five minutes after I entered the airport complex. I followed the appropriate signs and was headed for the "arrivals" area. I began to see caution signs warning vehicles of an upcoming clearance height. Having seen a million of these in my lifetime on overpasses, I paid little attention—not for one second recognizing the fact that I could be sitting in one such vehicle those signs were attempting to warn.

It should have become evident when I drove under a steel rectangle over the lane I was driving, in that it had little chains hanging from the overhead cross bar. I realized they were there for oversized vehicles, and I even acknowledged that it had to suck for them because, how would they navigate the remainder of this situation? Thankfully, not a problem I would have to face! Wrong. I went under the precautionary chains and felt them scrape across the solar panels on top of the van. In some moment of delusion and complete disregard, I convinced myself that the chains simply meant you were getting close to the clearance height, but since I didn't hit the actual steel crossbar, then I was good to go. So I kept driving. . . for like a hundred more feet. I came up to an area that appeared to be the reason for the chain-hanging warning that was now in my mirror.

I had already passed the chain test, so I approached slowly, optimistic that I would move right through and get to the arrivals gate in time to watch Nikki walk through the automatic sliding door. It is amazing, looking back now, how hard I was trying to convince myself I was right, knowing good and well this could turn into a huge cluster. At least my body knew. My back was soaking wet, I had to take my hat off because my head was sweating so bad, and the sun chose that moment to teach me about the intensity of the Southwest that I had been warned about. My heart was pounding.

At this point, I'm probably the only one left in the story who doesn't know I'm not going to make it. I inched up until I could no longer see the clearance overhang from my windshield. I thought maybe by some miracle I was good, until *WHAM!* Solid contact on the solar panels. It even jarred me a little. I would have sworn I was going less than one mile per hour, but it felt like I hit it at medium speed. The seatbelt locked and I felt it grab my chest. My mind wanted to stay calm, but my body wanted to panic. I'm honestly not sure which one of those won—it got blurry for a second after that—so I guess my body. And, I am not making this up, right at that moment I got a text from Nikki: "Just landed."

You have got to be freaking kidding me. I quickly sent back something along the lines of "trying to get there, cluster F out here, van too tall, might have to back down the highway." She immediately called me. She has no idea yet about the chains and all that, so I am allowing her to temporarily believe that this might not have been entirely orchestrated out of my ignorance.

By this time, I am painfully aware that everyone trying to pick up their loved one in the arrivals lane hates my guts. People swerving, flying by me, seemingly disgusted by my minor lapse in judgment. Simultaneously, I am on the phone with Nikki, assessing the situation, and sweating profusely, as the other motorists are going fifty miles per hour around me. My mind was blank. I think I was just hoping someone would roll by and tell me how to get out of this predicament. There was no obvious course of action. There were concrete barriers on either side of the three lanes of incoming traffic, with no pull-off or emergency lane, and no way I could physically proceed forward given the height of the van.

I felt the growing pressure that Nikki would soon be standing on the sidewalk. My van and I drove three thousand miles from South Carolina to Las Vegas to pick her up at this very spot. . . well, three quarters of a mile from this spot. I closed my eyes and took a deep breath.

Finally, either three hours or three minutes later—I have no idea, but it felt like forever—a kind gentleman stopped catty corner about thirty yards behind me to help me out. Our communication was initially restricted to expressions in my side mirror and hand gestures. I leaned out the window giving the "thanks for stopping to help, WTF do I do now" gesture. The man gestures that I should take action. I had no idea what action to take, so I gave back the "I don't know" gesture. Then he did the same thing but more emphatically. It's like when talking to a person who is deaf with only your voice. When they let you know they're deaf, you yell at them. Well, they're still deaf; they can't hear you. That is how I felt. . . *Sir, thank you for stopping; however, I still have no idea what to do.*

To help solve this barrier in communication, I decided to exit the van, and walk back toward the guy. This certainly helped his ability to communicate more effectively, because as I passed my taillights and came into his view, he gave me the unmistakable gesture of "WTF are you doing?" *Well, do you mean in general? Or the fact that I've landed myself in this harmless clearance debacle? Or WTF am I doing outside of my vehicle with cars whizzing by, horns blowing, middle fingers being magnetically lifted to full extension by the moon, after you gave me what felt to you like a clear solution of how to get myself out of this cluster?*

With that, I returned to the van, flipped the hazard lights on and threw her in reverse. I went as fast as I could toward his vehicle. As I approached him, he jumped in his car and sped off, completing his good deed for the day. Only problem was, I still wasn't far back enough to attempt a different route.

There was a turn-off across three lanes of traffic another twenty to thirty yards back. So, any moment I did not see a vehicle furiously rounding the curve, I inched back. It was terrifying. With my own rich history of texting and driving, it wasn't lost on me that any one of these sedans disguised as race cars could run up on me before realizing it. Once I was far enough to feel like I could make the turn, I threw on my blinker and started playing Frogger. I made it over the three lanes to a different ramp, which ended up being the ramp for the long-term parking lot. I felt sure long-term parking was OK for overheight vehicles until I came to another clearance bar. Why were there no signs? I know I cannot be the only person in a normal-height-looking but slightly-too-tall vehicle trying to pick someone up from the Las Vegas International Airport. Serious inquiry: Has anyone else ever had this problem here?

I knew I didn't fit, but once again convinced myself everything was fine and I could slip right under this bar and this F'd up game of pinball Frogger would be over. I did ease up to this one a little more slowly, just to give off the awareness that I was close when I slipped comfortably beneath it. I was probably within a second or two of this second simple math equation becoming a reality when another kind soul felt moved to come to my aid. I could identify who it was rather quickly by the fact that he was absolutely laying on the horn. We had no communication gap. He leaned out the window as far as he could with his foot still on the brake, and just gave me the Dikembe Mutombo finger wag. No, no, no, no!

Fortunately, I had been in this exact position as recently as three minutes ago, so I was familiar with the proper protocol. I turned on the emergency flashers, and threw her in reverse again. This probably lasted another six to seven minutes, which felt like two hours, until I could finally pull down a third ramp labeled "employees only."

While this charade was unfolding outside, Nikki was patiently waiting to deboard the plane when the lady next to her received a phone call. She had just hung up with me telling her that it was a disaster outside, that I had the entire traffic grid shut down, or some version of that. The lady next to Nikki told whoever she was talking to that it might be a minute before they deplane and she can get her bags to meet outside. The person on the phone responded, "well, it might take me a minute, too." All Nikki could think about was the person on the phone proceeding with something like, *Some idiot out here has the whole damn airport shut down, stopped in the middle of the road!* She got a good giggle out of that and thought to herself, *That's my idiot.*

The day before, I had locked my key in the van at a campground outside of Zion. I thought at the time, if that was the biggest hurdle I had to cross during this two-month jaunt across America, that would be a huge win. It took less than twenty-four hours for that not to be the case. I hoped this was not a developing trend for the remainder of the trip. Blunders are not an area of life where I hope to over-perform.

But who cares? I did something idiodic. Sue me. Spanx founder Sara Blakely often talks about the importance of getting embarrassed. Once you are comfortable being embarrassed, what is there left to fear? This is a challenging area for me, perhaps you too. Who are we trying to be perfect for? A whole bunch of other people who also aren't perfect? That doesn't make any sense. Laugh at the ridiculous episode and move on. That's what I kept telling myself, because I caught myself in this delusion that I had to perform everything exactly perfectly for Nikki while she was with me. Why? We had been dating for a few years. She is more informed than anyone else of my imperfections. She still loves me. Maybe even in part, those imperfections are *why* she loves me.

You're more than your worst moment

Taking it all in stride requires humility, acceptance, forgiveness, and grace. It requires that we offer all of those things to ourselves, and that is hard. Even in light-hearted examples like the Vegas airport story, I had to swallow my pride, back off of the unrealistic expectations I set for myself, accept the reality of the moment, and let it all go. I have often felt like I need to show that I am being hard on myself, or that I am dissatisfied with myself, simply to portray to others that I am actually better than this. How is that helpful?

I begin to justify why I did some ridiculous thing, or how it was not actually my fault. *If the signage would have been better at the airport. If the construction engineers and architects would have realized there are standard vehicles taller than eight feet. If people were not in such a rush, then all of this could have been avoided. It is clearly not my fault.* On and on and on. Who gives a shit? Whom do we actually need to prove our worthiness to? I tend to proceed as if it's other people who should be informed that I am better than this, when in fact, I am trying to prove it to myself.

It's easier for me to buy into "take it all in stride" when in reference to embarrassing blunders like the Vegas airport story. How about when the stakes are higher? When the repercussions are more severe? Are we able to go through something extremely difficult, process and accept it (in whatever amount of time necessary), and move forward? Or do we label and limit ourselves for the rest of our life because of something we have allowed to define us from years ago?

What if we were all defined by our worst moment? I learned about this from my friend Lester, who served a life sentence in prison for murder. At nineteen years old, Lester was involved in a drug deal gone bad when someone stole his supply, and Lester shot and killed him. Nothing I am going to say here is meant to justify his action, and he would be the first one to tell you that.

I met Lester when he was in his late forties, a few years after his release from prison. We met at an overnight orientation retreat for a leadership program. I didn't know anything about him, or the sixty-three other people in our cohort. All I knew was that we were all embarking on a ten-month journey of community service, leadership development, and a deeper understanding of the city in which we lived.

During an ice-breaker at the retreat, each person stood up and gave three interesting facts about themselves. Two weeks prior, I had completed my first official full marathon in Oklahoma City, so I couldn't wait to share this achievement in front of a crowd full of strangers, secretly hoping it might gain me some credibility. Others shared how many countries they have visited, how many languages they speak, impressive hobbies in art and performance. When it rolled around to Lester, I cannot remember the first two facts about him, but the third was a bomb dropped on the entire room. "I served a life sentence in prison for murder."

Silence. Fear. Concern. Uncertainty. You could hear a pin drop in this room full of dropped jaws until Lester broke the silence. With a grin and as calm as ever, the way only Lester can control a room, he said, "But don't worry, all of y'all are safe."

The tension was broken. The room broke out in laughter. Not at what Lester had done thirty years ago. There was a confidence in him, one that undoubtedly had been cultivated through unimaginable life experiences, acceptance, and growth.

Eventually I would learn of Lester's entire story, but first I was able to know Lester. I was quickly drawn to him by his humor, his passion, and his selflessness in serving others. I learned of his business endeavors, his incredibly moving speeches of redemption, and his advocacy work, impacting legislation at the local and state levels. He is a TEDx presenter and entrepreneur, has authored and published several books, and flies all over the country inspiring and moving companies and organizations toward meaningful change.

Taking it all in stride is not about avoidance, but about acceptance. About grace and courage. Lester avoided his feelings and emotions for many years of his life, which continued through the beginning of his prison sentence. He had blamed other people and difficult circumstances for his actions.

He talked about a time in prison when a chaplain gave him a book to read called *As A Man Thinketh* by James Allen. Lester had a seventh grade level in reading, so he was not interested in picking up this new habit. He told the chaplain he was going to die in prison; everyone had told him that since he arrived. The chaplain told him that's what *they* say; what about what *you* say? So, he read the book, which described the mind as a garden, that we are the gardener of our own mind. Plant good seeds, you get positive and healthy growth. Plant bad seeds and don't care for them, then nothing grows.

Reading that book led to many other books, and to an entirely re-structured and redirected mindset. Lester learned about gratitude. Even in prison, there were many things he became grateful for. He learned about having agency over his own decisions and the way he responded to things. If anyone could have mailed it in and accepted his fate with all of the cards stacked against them, it was Lester. But he refused to give in.

So, when I say take it all in stride, what I am really asking is: Are we able to accept an action or circumstance, and decide to move forward? Sure, some take more time than others, some appear to have less magnitude, but all take courage. Are you a person that defines yourself by your overall body of work? Or one that defines yourself by your worst moment?

When Lester was released from prison, his mentor told him to get a suit and go sit in a coffee shop. He told him that no one in that coffee shop knows anything about his life. No one knows what he did at nineteen years old. No one knows he just walked out of a prison after serving a life sentence. No one knows the transformation, the tears, the isolation, the torment, the self-discovery, none of that. Who do you believe yourself to be right now? That is who you are. As a person thinketh, so are they.

When our worst moments prompt us to change

Lester's story may be an extreme example, but it's easy to limit ourselves based on some label that has been placed on us. All of us have experienced some version of this story. I know I have. We also have the tendency at times to get in the mindset of waiting for the other shoe to drop, awaiting the next piece of bad news. *If life is going well, something bad is about to happen.* But if we build a solid foundation and begin to understand and trust ourselves, we are more equipped to handle things as they arise. Of course we may still experience anger, sadness, shock, or fear, but if we know who we are as a person, stand by our values, and are open to change, then we are prepared to bounce back from adversity and misfortune.

Nearly one year after the move to Nicaragua did not work out for me, a friend and I planned a white water rafting trip in the mountains of north Georgia. The same mountains where I spend my Advance in Solitude each year. The little mountain town where my grandparents were born and raised.

I had purchased a fifth wheel camper to live in, as a way to resist jumping back into the same life routine I previously had. So my friend and I took the camper up to the mountains to stay at a campground near the river launch site. We arrived at the campground on Friday in time to get everything set up and relax a little bit before dark.

The next morning we had an early start to the day, meeting at the outpost and gearing up for the day of rafting. This was a guided tour down the Chattooga River, with Class IV and V rapids covering about a seven-mile stretch of the river. The Chattooga is designated and protected as a Wild & Scenic river, which essentially means there is no construction of any kind, just you and nature. It is such a beautiful setting roaring down between the hills with creeks and waterfalls joining in along the way. The latter part of the rafting trip boasts the Five Falls, which is a series of five badass rapids in succession. It's a great grand finale of the trip.

The Chattooga is also the site of the filming of the movie *Deliverance*. Although most of the raft guides are not local to the region, it's still a big part of the experience to educate their customers on significant scenes from the movie. They will point out creeks and rocks and banks where certain scenes took place, even what they typically call "the love scene."

After lunch by a waterfall and racing through the five falls, we ended the trip with a nice, calm float across a small lake to the take out point. An incredible day, so much fun in nature with my friend in a place I love. We headed back to the camper to process the experience over a nice cold beverage. I had my guitar, the campsite was situated perfectly amongst the trees of the foothills, and the weather was perfect.

As the afternoon moved toward evening, we drove over into town for some supper and social interaction. We chose a restaurant that was a converted filling station, and when the weather is nice they open the bay doors to a huge outdoor seating area. A band was playing in the small, covered pavilion, and people were dancing, eating, and having a good time.

We talked to people as they came up to the bar where we were sitting to order their drinks. Turns out, a nearby smaller town had bussed in a group of people to hang out for the evening. Everyone seemed to be enjoying themselves, and the energy was infectious. As the evening progressed, we met several people who lived locally, so I played the name game with them to see if they knew any of my family members. Being that it is a small town, and I am related to about half of it, there were certainly some mutual connections.

It's always exciting to connect to this part of my past that holds such fond memories. This trip was before I started the annual Advance in Solitude, so it had been many years since I spent significant time in the area, yet I always held it in high regard. Most likely because of the love my grandparents had for the place where they grew up.

The night was winding down and the band was finished playing, and our new friends asked us if we wanted to go across the street to a brand new rooftop bar. I'm pretty sure this was a dry county when I was a child, and now they have a rooftop bar? No way we could pass up that opportunity. We enjoyed our time up there with our new friends with several stories, laughs, and shots.

There is a vague recollection of a round of Jager Bombs and one of our new friends asking, "how are y'all getting home?" Well, that was a good question, one we had not yet given appropriate attention to. Being on the rooftop, we could see two locations in the town that had active traffic checks, so our new friend urged us to address this dilemma. A quick Google search came back with two cab companies in the area. Both closed. No worries, Uber and Lyft were solid options—until we realized neither of those services existed in this small mountain town. Our friends got quite a laugh that we even considered the massively popular global apps.

It was a no-brainer. I would do what I have done hundreds, if not thousands, of times before. We walked down the stairs, crossed the street, and hopped in my truck to drive home. I can't remember why, but we sat in the truck for a few minutes, maybe to gather ourselves, before we backed out of the parking spot. The more likely reason was that we had to find the perfect song to set the vibe for the ride back.

Our campsite was about seven miles from town, a couple of quick traffic lights, then a rural, windy, two-lane road across the mighty Chattooga River back into the South Carolina side. We made it about three quarters of a mile, through the first traffic light, before we got pulled over by Officer Buchanan. It didn't take him long to strongly suggest I step out of the vehicle. Another vehicle with flashing blue lights pulled up on our six. I don't know everything about traffic stops, but I do know when an additional officer of the law joins the party, it is not a favorable situation. The effect of the Jager was suddenly gone, and my friend and I were both vividly aware this was not going our way.

Officer Buchanan was cordial, the second officer less so. I refused the Breathalyzer and field sobriety test. Not that I believed it to be a big challenge, but because I remembered that being the recommendation of several attorneys I had talked to over the years. As a formality, Buchanan placed me in handcuffs and situated me at the hood of my truck. After refusing to participate in the game and activity session of the traffic stop, the second officer started letting me have it. "Do you know what we can give you for all of this?" No sir. "Did you know that this is a felony in the state of Georgia?" Well, no sir, I didn't, I live in South Carolina. "Well, you're in Georgia now! It's your responsibility to know the laws and re-percussions when you are in this state!"

OK, quick poll: Who reads the entire book of laws when they enter another state? Is it even called a book of laws? A code? I have no idea. When I drove my van across America, I went through twenty-five states. If you were me, would you have become well-versed in every single law within each of these states? Not typically known as a master of preparation, I only started packing my van the day before I left. It would have taken me six months to read all of this. The VanAm trip was not even a definite six months prior to departure.

I'm not saying I should not take responsibility for my actions. I just thought this officer's line of questioning was ridiculous. I did not argue. I did not question his knowledge of the book of laws. Matter of fact, I barely said anything. There was not much for me to say. Very aware of the predicament, I was simply willing to accept my fate. The second the field test and Breathalyzer were refused, I knew that I was headed to the Rabun County jail. We would figure out all the details later, but right then, I was going in. Eventually, when the second cop was probably about to lose his voice, he let me be. They both walked over to have some words with my friend that I was not privy to.

As I was uncomfortably leaned up against the hood of my truck in handcuffs, I realized exactly where I was standing. The patrol car lights were flashing in my eye, and just up the hill, with every blue flicker, I could see my grandparents' mountain cabin where I used to frequent as a child. The adrenaline of the stop wore off, and sadness overcame my body. I felt a series of tears rolling down my cheeks and into my beard.

Earlier in the book I told how we would sit on the porch of that moun-tain house and listen to people place their orders at McDonald's on my Pa's ham radio. We could also hear police scanners of traffic stops. Traffic stops just like this one.

Not only was the structure on that hill a significant reminder of joyful childhood experiences, so too were the two people who made it all possible, my grandparents. I had been thinking about Pa a lot that weekend. He just passed away less than three months before, after a long and excruciating fight with Alzheimer's. I had written a song for him, and I was able to sing it for him the night before, at the top of my lungs. Just me, my guitar, and the mountains where he grew up. I am not a talented singer, or guitarist for that matter, but none of that was important.

I had thought of him earlier in the day when my friend and I went up to the old mountain house. We walked out on that same back porch, only to find it barely attached and standing, and covered in kudzu. To see the house so weathered and uninhabitable is a clear symbol of the seasons of life. Standing there at this moment, looking up at the old house, I am afraid, and more than anything, I am disappointed.

Officer Buchanan walked calmly back over breaking my pity party and loaded me in the back of his car. We drove off. I told him of my grandparents and that mountain house on the whole ride to the jail.

By the time I was transported, checked in, and assigned my lodging for the night, it was probably 2 am. I was put in a room with another individual who was obviously fast asleep. Well, not for long. All of the nerves of the past couple of hours had me needing to use the facilities. Once I finished my business in this tiny square block room, I attempted to wash my hands in the steel sink, setting off a continuous, high pressure stream of water directly into the middle of our floor. My celly, who had not yet acknowledged my existence, jumped out of the bed and over to the sink and simply cupped his hands over the water spout, allowing the water to fall right into the trough until it timed out a few seconds later.

So now, on a damp blanket on the floor with a disgruntled bunkmate, I try to get some sleep. Impossible. The sadness from the events of the evening reigned triumphant over sleep and any other potential thought or feeling I may have encountered. The sadness, expressed as disappointment, then teetered back and forth over to anger. This was a low point in my life, unquestionably.

How can I take this in stride? I had worked so hard to make drastic improvements over the past decade, and now I was right back at ground zero. *Was it all for nothing? Had I been fooling myself into thinking I have evolved into a refined iteration of my former good-for-nothing, never-gon-na-be-anybody self?* Is this series of questioning familiar to you? Do you relate and identify more with your low points than your wins? This is everything! How do you respond in these situations? Do you believe yourself to be—no, define yourself as—the person ramming the bar at the Vegas airport, the person who shot someone thirty years ago, the person laying on the floor of a jail cell staring up at the ceiling? Are you defined by your worst moment?

All of these, plus whatever comes to mind for you, are a piece of your whole story. A part of what makes you the person you are. They are all situations to navigate in life. Life situations, not your life! What do you tell a friend when they find themselves down, when they have a blunder, or have made a painful mistake? You tell them to keep going! What do you tell yourself? *Keep going!* You did not come this far just to come this far. Keep going.

Laying on that plastic tub on the floor of the jail cell that night, I remember thinking, *Maybe I should take a couple of weeks off from drinking, just to make sure my priorities are in order.* Yes, I was down on myself. Yes, I was sad. I felt a great deal of guilt, embarrassment, and shame. *And* I felt hope. That was a new response for me. It was a result of putting in all of that work, and going through the steps laid out in this book. It was not back to ground zero, not this time. Something was different now, whether I recognized it or not.

How your response to bad situations can alter your life

A week flew by. I was easily abstaining from drinking, still visibly shaken by what had happened, and trying not to let anyone else in on the secret. The second week, a much greater challenge. I was set to attend a huge work event on Hilton Head Island, where we had customers, vendors, and colleagues coming in from all across the country to attend the Heritage Golf Tournament. It is a massive party. There were self-imposed and external expectations that I let loose. But it's way more obvious when someone is *not* drinking at an event like this, than when they are. I knew I would be exposed, but I could do it.

I was likely the only person who did not have a sip of alcohol the entire weekend. It was shaky, it was difficult, but I made it. After two weeks without hangovers, I was still energized and encouraged, and probably still slightly in fear of what will happen with my citations. My court date was a few months out, and I didn't know if I would lose my license, or what other repercussions lay ahead. During the traffic stop, the second officer had quite aggressively informed me that one of my many citations was a felony in the state of Georgia, so that was anxious territory on a whole different level. If I could make it until my court date without drinking, that would be a substantial accomplishment.

Thankfully, I made it. At my court appearance, I see Officer Buchanan in the lobby, still too embarrassed to speak with him. The ruling did not necessarily go in my financial favor, but I believe it went in my legal favor. One hundred hours of community service and six months probation. All manageable. Immediately, I began thinking of areas of interest within the city where I live as possible locations to serve. I also thought of how cool it would be, and surprising, if I could continue not drinking until all of my hours had been served.

The first location I tried appeared to be a good fit. I could pick the day, and work four-hour shifts at a time, a nice chunk to whittle down the one hundred overall hours. But it did not feel purposeful. I knew I was going through the motions to fulfill a court requirement based on a poor decision. But it just did not feel right. I love the community where I live, and it was important to me to make an impact. So I began looking elsewhere.

A friend used to serve breakfast at a local homeless shelter and said she would join me on my shifts if I was interested. I was in. The shifts were only an hour and a half long, so I would have to work many more days to reach my community service requirements. In a few short weeks, I forgot about the hours. I wanted to show up to serve breakfast, I was engaged, and I felt like I could make an impact. If I had to guess, I've logged four hundred hours of volunteer time at that place. The point is not to say "look at me." I found purpose there. Something bigger than getting slapped with a hefty requirement of my time because of one shitty night. I was vulnerable and open to change, and as a result was impacted deeply through the experience of spending time there.

By the time the hours were fulfilled, I still had a couple of months of probation left. *Hell with it, surely I can make it until then without drinking.* I made it nine months. *What if I can make it ONE YEAR without taking a sip of alcohol?* It would feel almost like a miracle. I have never gone more than a couple of weeks over the past twenty years, and that's being generous, more likely it was one week.

My friend and I were pulled over by Officer Buchanan and his comrade on April 13, 2019. As I am writing this, it has been more than six years since the last time I drank a sip of alcohol. Engagement, openness to change, presence, digging deep into my emotional depths, and developing and understanding my true values. That night in north Georgia was terrible. But the building blocks I had laid, every piece of this book, culminated in the ability to make it something completely new. It changed the trajectory of my life forever. Because I was able to accept it, learn from it, address it, and bust my ass to make sure I got to a better spot.

We do not have the benefit of knowing exactly how the dots will connect in our future. We can, however, look back to see how they have connected to get us where we are today. I encourage you to partake in the exercise of reflection. It's neat, funny even at times, to really dive into what brought us to this point. Since that day, in addition to not drinking,

I took up distance running and completed two full marathons and seven ultra-marathons. In the ten-month leadership program where I met Lester, I was voted by my classmates as the most impactful leader, and was the class lead on our community service project. Oh yeah, guess where we chose to do our project—the same homeless center where I served my court-ordered community services two years prior. I served breakfast there for two years, and then showed up with sixty-five friends to help transform their facilities and service offerings.

Eventually, I went back up to north Georgia. Back to the same hill where I played as a kid with my siblings, sitting on the mountain house porch with my grandparents. The same hill I saw in the flashing of Officer Buchanan's patrol car lights. I went back with pride and gratitude. I went back to build two new mountain houses on that property, each named after one of my grandparents. A line from the song I wrote my Pa, which I played for him the night before I got arrested and taken to jail, goes:

> *If we could have just one conversation, I wonder what I would learn.*
>
> *And if we had that one conversation, would you be proud of what I've become?*

That question plagued me as I was laying in Rabun County jail. But I no longer have to wonder what Pa's answer would have been. I have full confidence in his response, due in large part to *my* response to the situation. Because I was able to take it all in stride.

Step Outside of Your Comfort Zone

Face discomfort and grow

The steps in this book, either alone or in succession, can be extremely difficult. It is not easy to pursue a new and improved version of yourself. Growth is challenging, at times painful, even. There is fear, resistance, setbacks, and uncertainty. All of those suck and can be scary. Many people stop at the discomfort and retreat. But don't you want to advance? I know I do.

Where taking it all in stride is about acceptance and response to external stimuli, stepping outside of your comfort zone is an extension of that. It is about acceptance to external *and* internal stimuli, and about taking initiative. It's really an extension of engaging, because that section was based around taking action. Now we are talking about taking that action with more intention, understanding, clarity, confidence, and trust. Engagement created the momentum. It got the ball rolling. Then through understanding your emotions and leaning into your values, you have gained confidence in who you are as a person. You are now open to change, internal and external. You focus on what you can control, and when those things you cannot control arise, you take it in stride and keep going.

You are fully equipped to enter uncharted territory intentionally and on purpose. You have already stepped outside of your comfort zone to get to this point undoubtedly. Take a minute (or thirty) to reflect on some of the toughest things you have gone through, some of the challenges you took on thinking you would not come out on the other side. Guess what? You are here. You made it through. You have made it through every challenge previously set before you. Think about that!

What are those times for you? And what was the outcome? How did you feel after you did the thing that took you out of comfort? Was it worth it? Did you grow? Are you now better for it? Nearly all of the time, the answer is yes.

With this type of data, it seems like a no-brainer to continue to put yourself out of comfort, but the reality is that it is a new challenge each time. It can become a habit that is created, and in that sense "easier" over time, but if the goal or challenge becomes easy, it is by definition no longer stepping outside of your comfort zone. What is scary and uncomfortable today will likely not be as scary and uncomfortable this time next year.

How cool is that? That is expansion. That is growth, and it allows room for continued growth, which is only possible with a continued willingness and intention to be vulnerable and to lean into discomfort.

This section's realization could also have been titled Get into Your Growth Zone, because that is the goal. And, as has been true with other realizations in this book, all time spent outside of the comfort zone is not created equal. All discomfort is not created equal. To best understand this, I always picture an illustration that Nicole Griffin uses in her coaching program, Grounded in your Growth Zone. Picture it as three concentric circles. The innermost circle is the comfort zone. From the edge of the comfort zone out to the next line is the growth zone. Then beyond that to the outer edge of the drawing is overwhelm.

We all know what overwhelm feels like. It stinks. It's difficult to successfully complete tasks, and our bodies and minds feel out of whack. Our nervous system is dysregulated. No matter how hard we try, we feel like we are not able to accomplish anything. Many times, we respond to this by trying to go harder. That does not work. Everything in life is about balance, and this is no different. You have to be the judge of where you are at a given point in time. Today the answer may be to lean harder into discomfort to explore the endless world of growth possibilities. Or today you might be firmly in overwhelm, and what serves you best is to rest and recalibrate. The more in touch we are with our intuition, the easier it becomes to navigate this fluctuation.

Once in the growth zone, you might begin to recognize if or when you are approaching either the comfort zone or overwhelm. Redirect, and swim the other way for a bit. It is a moving target, and your position within the model varies over time. However, presence, mindfulness, recognizing emotions, and reflection all certainly come to our aid in maintaining a healthy position of growth.

When in overwhelm, take time to recognize why you are there. Have you changed your routine or neglected one of your positive coping strategies? It's OK. Today is a good time to re-implement it. Has life been hectic lately and have you running around like a chicken with its head cut off? OK, can you carve out *any* time to do one small thing that you loved to do as a kid? Can you initiate an interaction with a friend you haven't talked with or seen in a while? Those might feel like another task to complete, but these are for *you*. I believe you can make it work.

Now for the flip side: Are you stuck in your comfort zone? Or do you feel like you are happily inside of your comfort zone? Perhaps that can hold true for periods of time, but as time moves forward, too much time inside of comfort turns into regret, resentment, and untapped potential. The thing that moves me out of my comfort zone is the terrifying, mind-numbing thought of never realizing my potential. All of the things we say we want to accomplish, or that we plan to do some time in the future, take place outside of the comfort zone. So denying yourself movement into discomfort robs you of the opportunity to explore potential areas of growth.

Staying in the comfort zone does not make you less likely to face discomfort. Less likely to be able to handle it, perhaps. The area of discomfort expands, making your comfort zone smaller and smaller over time, as your resiliency weakens. Conversely, the more you step outside of your comfort zone, gain exposure, and engage in challenges, the larger your comfort zone grows.

The goal here is not to beat yourself up or inflict punishment, physical or mental, if you feel dissatisfied with your position in one of these zones. It's an opportunity to reflect and create awareness—and acceptance, which we have talked about throughout this book. Specifically in this case, self-acceptance.

Once you shift your mindset and look forward to stepping outside of your comfort zone, it becomes incredibly exciting. As with being open to change, the opportunities are endless. What you can actually accomplish is endless. You begin to realize your body and mind are capable of going to lengths you never before imagined. When your body and mind get to that previously inconceivable place, you take a breath and think, *what's next?* Nothing gets me going more than that feeling. Keep going.

Often people say to me: "Oh, you ran an ultramarathon? I could never do that!" Bullshit. If you want to, you can do it. They mean it as a compliment, and I get it. Maybe they don't actually want to do it. That's OK, too. But if you really want to do it, there is only one thing standing in your way: *you.* I haven't nearly tapped into my full potential, and neither have you. Interests change, professional and personal goals fluctuate, life situations flip the script on all of us, but we still have potential. Damn, that is inspiring. Advance.

It's never too late to learn what leads to Future You

After my arrest that night in north Georgia, I continued to feel a forceful pull to the area. Yes, something bad happened there, but I was able to take it in stride and turn it into something positive. I built two cabins on the land where my grandparents' old mountain house stood. I could not be more proud of them, and that they were built in Nana and Pa's honor. What isn't talked about a lot is how close it was to never happening. How many times I almost quit. Admittedly, I am not the most fiscally responsible human ever created, and like many others, I get nervous when larger amounts of money are in question. Building two cabins simultaneously qualified for me as a large amount of money.

I have become used to taking physical risks and pushing my body past limits previously believed, but this was a new category. *The cabins are three hours away from where I live, so how can I manage construction? How do I decide who is going to build them, what to build, and if any of this even makes any sense at all?* This was so far outside of my comfort zone it made me sick to my stomach simply thinking about it.

There are many realizations in this book that I leaned into in order to get those cabins built. I did not need to know how to rent them out on Airbnb before the land was graded. Take small chunks, and engage. As Posner said, step one is to take one step. Of course, the arrest was emotional, for several reasons, but there were many emotions afterward as well. I felt so attached to this specific area, to the hill we played on as kids with an old, perfect mountain house on it. My emotions, and understanding them, helped fuel my commitment to taking that project on.

My values even played a role. Building the cabins allowed me to reconnect with family members and build meaningful relationships with them. It would be a huge achievement for this project to come to fruition, and since I identified my emotional inspiration, what would be the cost of not ever starting?

Being open to change and taking things in stride. Holy moly, this project was eaten up with both. It just so happened that, once I actually stepped so far out of my comfort zone and decided to do it, choose a builder, and grade the land, COVID hit. Prices soared, material became impossible to acquire, and the timeline for building doubled. But guess what? We made it. They got built, I stay in them and rent them out, and my entire family has been able to use them as well. Stepping out of the zone of comfort can take on many different looks, and this was expansion and growth with a payoff that can't hold a price tag.

What have you been continuously putting off because you can always find a good reason *not* to do it? Man, we can talk ourselves out of anything. We have become so used to saying "no" that it has developed into a habit. Of course, there are times we need to say no and prioritize our time and energy in directions that best serve us. This is different. This is about saying no to the things we want most but are too scared to step outside of our comfort zone and go after.

No matter how old you are today, you might have wanted to start younger. Understandable, but today is the youngest you will ever be. Eleanor Roosevelt said: "Today is the oldest you've ever been, and the youngest you'll ever be again." How exciting! You have never before had more cumulative experience and knowledge than you have right this very second. At the same time, you will never have the same level of youth that you have today. So act, get outside of your comfort zone and chase what speaks directly to *you* in your soul.

I think about this idea all of the time, and use it to talk myself into all sorts of things. Dance classes, songwriting, ultra running, learning sign language, changing careers, going on an epic adventure. When I hear my inner voice say, *ahh man, maybe you're too old to be doing this*. Maybe? Well, if maybe so, then also maybe not! If you feel uncertain you are too old now, I can tell you that you won't be any younger ten years from now.

What even is "too old"? Nobody told Alfredo Aliaga he was too old when he hiked the Grand Canyon rim to rim at ninety-two years old. Actually, I'm sure they did tell him he was too old, and he did that shit anyway! Diana Nyad was not too old at sixty-four years old to be the first person to ever swim the one hundred ten miles from Cuba to Florida without a shark cage, and she did it on her fifth attempt. Yuichiro Miura climbed Mount Everest at eighty.

These examples may seem extreme, but what have you always wanted to do? There was no reason my sister could not try out for the Atlanta Falcons cheerleading team months before her fortieth birthday. Professional cheer has been a lifelong dream of hers. She might regret not trying out at twenty-five, but she won't live another day wishing she would have given it a shot. The ripple effect on her children and those around her is immeasurable. She is now a different person having given it a shot.

At forty years old, I decided to embark on a journey in a seemingly unrelated field and enter a master's program in rehabilitation counseling. This is after being in industrial sales for nearly twenty years. The money was great, and the people within my organization were great. The comfortable thing to do was to keep right on trucking until retirement. But I knew that was not enough for me. I knew that I would regret not trying something different, and resent my inaction for the rest of my life.

College was not what you would call a strength of mine the first go round. It was a struggle to get invested in the process because I had not found my area of interest. After attending four colleges in four years, I finally buckled down and got serious enough to see the light at the end of the tunnel. I graduated in five years plus a summer. For nearly two decades I swore I would never register for another college class, and here I was applying for a three-year master's program in a field I knew nothing about at forty. Thankfully I had become open to change and ready to engage. But this was still way outside of my comfort zone.

During the interview, they asked questions about undergrad that had been long since forgotten. I couldn't even find my transcript, and when it came to vaccinations, my alma mater had no records of me. That is how long it had been since I was last in college. Once the classwork started, I was in classes with people fresh out of undergrad: twenty-two and twenty-three year olds. How in the world could I relate? Am I the weird, old guy? Will I be able to keep up?

New stuff is hard. But I was built for it. I was vulnerable and I engaged. I took the leap. I was open to change, and when the classwork actually started I dived all the way in head first. I was present and mindful. Often, the things we embark on feel like disconnected, individual, unrelated events, but they aren't.

Had I not gotten pulled over by Officer Buchanan, I never would have stopped drinking, and I never would have volunteered at the homeless center. If I didn't stop drinking, I never would have applied for the leadership program where I met the sixty-five incredible leaders of my community. I actually applied once and didn't get accepted. The only reason I applied the next year, mere minutes before the deadline, was because I made a promise to Transitions Homeless Center that I would do everything in my power to help them.

I stood on a stage at the leadership retreat and poured my heart out about my experience with sobriety and my experience working with the people at Transitions. I cried. No, I balled. Those people rallied around me and chose me to lead the community service project. Had it not been for the relationships built with those amazing leaders, I never would have had the confidence and courage to apply for a master's program and make the difficult decision to leave such a great career. Every single one of those things were so far outside of my comfort zone, and by stepping out there I am following my dreams and continuously tapping into opportunities I never could fathom.

REALIZATION

Live in Concert with Your Situation

Pay attention to your life

It is so easy for us to hide behind the belief that we are doing all we do for others. How selfless, we think. We feel good about ourselves when we help other people. It might even feel like it offers us purpose or a life's mission. It makes it way less scary to act on what we believe to be the best interests of someone else.

People pleasers do not like this quote from record producer and author Rick Rubin: "The audience comes last. I believe that. I'm not making it for them. I'm making it for me. And it turns out that when you make something truly for yourself, you're doing the best thing you possibly can for the audience."

So, how about acting in the best interest of *you*? How about showing up as *you*? It is not selfish. It benefits everyone around you. The audience comes last, and that is with the utmost respect and benefit to the audience.

When you are whole internally, you no longer have to hang onto the reactions, behaviors, and decisions of others. You are not dependent on those you serve. They are not in charge of your emotions, feelings, behaviors, decisions, reactions, or worth. *You* are. As a result, you are now of the best service to them.

Plants bear the best fruit when they are at their healthiest: when they are watered, exposed to sun, and thriving. Have you ever seen a tomato plant that stays in the dark, gets no water, and is in poor soil? It tries like hell to produce tomatoes. It wants to, it feels like it is what it is supposed to do, but it has no strength. When we stretch ourselves dangerously thin and continuously put ourselves at the back of the line, we are of no value to anyone else.

When we live in true authenticity, the opposite is true. When you show up as the truest form of yourself, your heart, soul, and spirit are fueled by simply being you. You can show up in any situation, unapologetically. You only have one life, and it is not selfish one bit to prioritize yourself. You do not owe anything to anyone else.

This is a celebration. A culmination of all of the work you have put in, and also a celebration that you have full autonomy and permission to enter any situation and act as you. Nothing is more satisfying and inspiring than that. The content of this book is simply a foundation, possibly a framework, to help spark thought as to what this looks like for your life. You now possess the confidence you have been yearning for. Step out there. Mess up. Try something crazy. Fall flat on your face. Pick yourself up, and get back in there. Call someone you haven't talked to in a while. Change your appearance. Take a trip. Learn to dance, paint, or make pottery. Pick up an instrument. Walk around the block. Do any and all of these things confidently and be proud you are doing them as an expression of your heart and soul.

Through engagement, momentum is created, and you have got the wheels turning. Intentional quality time with self and others brings life to the engagement. Presence and mindfulness reveal meaning within your interactions. Allowing yourself to feel your emotions highlights your uniqueness. Identifying and understanding your values guides decision making. With an openness to change and an acceptance of impermanence, possibilities never before imagined have now come into your view. When roadblocks arise, you are ready to handle them appropriately, take them in stride, and keep going. Ready to step outside of your comfort zone, and know that no matter what situation arises, you are ready. Because you are whole.

Remember the Eckhart Tolle quote from the beginning of the book. No matter where you are, who you are with, what your circumstances are, your life is right now. I agree with Eckhart Tolle one hundred percent. I also believe it is difficult for many people to separate the two, including me. So, I wrote this book. Thinking of living in concert with my situation helps me to conceptualize it. When acting in authenticity, the situation is secondary. The situation might dictate what action I take, but not why I take it. There is no dependence on the situation; rather, an independence on how you exist within a given situation.

Live in concert. Everyone has their own unique taste in music, but there is a shared understanding in how that music makes us feel. To me, there is nothing like taking in the atmosphere of one of your favorite artists playing live. Close your eyes. You are at a show of your favorite artist. They are playing all of your favorite songs. The movement of your body in perfect harmony with the pulse of the speakers. No one is watching and everyone is watching. Nothing matters and everything matters. You are in this one place, and simultaneously every place you have ever been before. You are a part of the concert; and equally, the concert is a part of you. Now and forever.

It is the world existing in perfect harmony. The energy of the setting, whether it be a stadium of a hundred thousand or the intimacy of a coffee shop. The energy of the artist, pouring every ounce of passion from the depth of their soul into a piece of art they have created. Time slows down, pressures and expectations disappear, and you are exactly where you are meant to be. Movement, joy, connection, peace, understanding, alignment. Presence.

That is what I visualize when I hear Eckhart Tolle's words about paying attention to life. Being fully immersed in the moment. But only rarely are we able to live the experience of this concert—or are we? What if we are able to exist in every situation as if it were with the same harmony as what you envisioned when you closed your eyes? This is congruence.

Live in concert with your situation. If you are on an out-of-town work assignment that you would rather not take, are you able to explore interests in the place you have traveled? A major league ballpark, a local 5K, a foodie tour. Are you able to take a book that you would not have been able to read at home due to coaching tee ball? Can you reflect on exactly what makes home so special?

Live in concert with your situation. Maybe you are in a role you do not love, but are working toward something bigger. Great. Your life does not have to be on hold until you reach the promotion. Explore passions and interests outside of work. Bring your quirkiness to the role you are currently occupying. Initiate a club, group, or afterwork meetup to build camaraderie, connection, and synergy.

Live in concert with your situation. If you are in a job you have continuously disliked for a year or more, leave that job. Put the steps in place to get out of there and pursue something that fulfills you. "I will just suck it up for nine more years until I retire." NO! Nine years? Your life is now, remember? Refuse to compromise *you*, and that is in the highest service to your family, your future endeavors, and everyone you have the potential to impact on this planet.

Live in concert with your situation. If you are single and know that you have so much to give to a relationship and a future with someone, that is outstanding. In the meantime, do not sit around and wait. Your life is now. The thing you have been in search of will likely be a byproduct of relentlessly pursuing your true authentic self. I know from experience.

Live in concert with your situation. Conversely to the previous, if you are in a relationship that has consistently and repetitively made you feel less than, worthless, inadequate, incapable, or in a constant state of misery, leave. Exit the relationship. Your life is now. *Your* life, the one and only of them that you get. It might not be your partner's fault; they might not be a bad person. You could have grown in different directions, or outgrown the nature of the relationship. All valid, and the answer remains the same.

Live in concert with your situation. Even when your life situation is downright shitty. You are still you, and your life is still now. Yes, it sucks, and you may feel the difficult emotions far more often than the fun ones, but you are not finished. Keep going. Sit outside and call a cousin, niece, or grandchild. Put on your best outfit. You are needed in this world, and you are needed as *you*.

Live in concert with your situation.

You are not behind

This phrase, living in concert with your situation, came to me while on my VanAm road trip. It was amazing to break free from the doubters and nay-sayers, and actually decide to take the two-month exploration of the nation. But then what? Could I allow myself to untie the thread of expectation that plagues our lives? It is what we are conditioned for. What was the best part? Did it live up to everything you thought it would be? Those questions were coming from others, and also from within. *Am I doing it all wrong? How do I rate this trip? How do I determine success?*

It's a funny thing about life, that the trip is never about the destination. VanAm was a microcosm of life in this way, whatever "thing" we are going to see or do becomes secondary. But only if we allow it to. Leaning into the realizations in this book allowed me to experience all of it. They came to me, some in a rush, and some in slow, gentle subtlety, in towns I cannot remember, and places I'll never forget.

The thought of writing this book never once crossed my mind while on the trip, though the seeds planted over time in my mind found the perfect environment for cultivation. Living in concert with my situation. I began typing words on a page a few months after my return, but I have been writing this book my whole life.

While on VanAm, I had the benefit of having no set destination. Outside of a couple of races scheduled, I had ultimate flexibility in location, duration, and direction. So, I was literally forced to focus on the journey and not the destination. Each stop its own, and also a part of one big, beautifully connected work of art. Sometimes I was in a city, and more often I was in rural areas. In each, I made a commitment to engage. My preference is the national parks and rural areas, but my situation did not always land me there, and I am grateful. If I would have been close-minded and only done the things in my comfort zone that I wanted to do most, so many experiences would have been robbed of me. A foodie tour in Denver, the strip in Vegas, Pier 39 in San Francisco, brisket in Kansas City, a Twins game in Minneapolis.

We talked earlier about the difficulties of managing expectations while engaging on an adventure like this: presence, appreciating impermanence, and quality interactions of engagement all aid the pressures of those expectations. It is the same in life. We do not have the opportunity to relive moments more than once. That can feel heavy, but to me, it also feels peaceful and freeing. Because my experiences are my own, and each is a part of something much larger. Just as yours are. Lean into the imperfection and impermanence, and offer yourself some grace to simply be.

Your experiences do not need to be just like someone else's to be valid or amazing. There is no way to compare my visit to Theodore Roosevelt National Park with anyone else's. Of course, I am happy to offer feedback and suggestions, as well as listen to others', but my situation was mine, yours is yours; act accordingly. The same goes for the other twenty-odd National Park Service sites I visited. Your trip might look completely different. Maybe you want to attend a game at all of the major league ballparks, run a race in each state, summit the high points, or visit museums. Your trip might not even be a trip. It might be something local, intellectual, professional, spiritual. It doesn't matter, show up authentically as you.

Doing so is a separator by every measure, because no one else is just like you. I love this quote by entrepreneur and investor Naval Ravikant: "You can escape competition through authenticity when you realize no one can compete with you on being you." Think about that. You can escape competition. So much of our lives today are consumed with comparison, stacking up, and feeling behind. Behind what? Behind who? Whatever "it" is, and whoever "they" are, cannot compete with you at being you! Run your own race. March to the sound of your own instrument. Live in concert with your situation.

Now let's talk about imposter syndrome. I was recently speaking to a group of college students at a men's empowerment seminar. The session I led was on identifying values and using the dimensions of wellness as a way to build self-confidence, resilience, and accountability. I was also part of a panel discussion speaking on questions and topics of self-care, boundaries, goal-setting, and mentorship. But the thing that reared its head the most, when the students asked questions, boiled down to imposter syndrome.

My first response is that we all have it. The older I get, the easier it is for me to see that is actually true. It's tough to accept or conceptualize when we see someone who appears to be light years ahead of us. The fear of inadequacy is very valid and normal. Of course, using coping tools and building skills help us to respond better, so developing those are critical. And I told them that imposter syndrome might not entirely go away, certainly not if we are willing to continue to step outside of our comfort zone. At first that sounds terrifying, that it does not go away, like it never gets better. But the peace I find in that is we are all on an equal playing field from that standpoint. You are good enough, you are capable, you are ready to start. Right now.

As Naval said, by being yourself you can escape competition. You can escape comparison because whoever you are comparing yourself to is *not you*. They have different circumstances, variables, and life experiences. They are likely dealing with other challenges that might not be apparent to you. Your unique skill set sets you apart from them, just as much as you think someone else's skill set sets them apart from you. You can escape imposter syndrome the same way. Perfectionism, anxiety, imposter syndrome, and comparison can all be escaped by living in concert with your situation. Your life is now.

The final question on the panel discussion was: "What is one piece of advice you would give your college self?" My initial thought was to not drink so much, although my college-aged self would definitely not have listened. Then I wrote down four words in all caps across the piece of scratch paper sitting in front of me. I lifted it, turned it around and showed it to the audience:

YOU ARE NOT BEHIND.

You are not behind. You're not. You are exactly where you should be, right now. That might not be where you want to be, and it is likely not where you used to be, but it is where you are. Your life is now. Do not allow comparison and fear to take that from you. Live in concert with your situation.

Being yourself in every situation

There isn't always the opportunity to take a two-month van trip across America in order to show that you are living in concert with your situation. More often, they will likely be seemingly less dramatic expressions of authentic living. It's OK. A little done often makes much. Your situation is specific to you, but I will offer a couple of examples that could spark some ideas.

As I entered a master's program at forty, unrelated to my previous career, I decided confidently on my own unique approach. My first go-round twenty years prior was an absolute slug fest. I was a terrible student, and it was a modern miracle that I actually graduated. But this time, I was interested in the content. I decided that no matter what, I was going to engage in the program and be an active participant in class discussions, be vulnerable, and maximize my experience by making it my own.

When an assignment was given, I took full creative license on putting my spin on it. For better or worse, they were going to get something that was fully mine. I figured it would either go exceptionally well or crash and burn, but either way I would be proud of expanding my mind and expressing my creativity.

In my first semester, I had an assignment where we were to video record ourselves with mock clients as if it were a true clinical counseling setting. This was to be able to review our posture, disposition, and conversation skills. To help make us comfortable, the first video was just a conversation with a friend of ours to get us a little more familiar with being on camera.

It was just a twenty minute requirement, so I could have gotten nearly anyone I know to do me a solid and complete the assignment. But that is not why I was there. I was there to learn and engage. I called my friend Taylor, who lived an hour and a half away from me. I asked, if I drove up one evening during the week, would he mind recording a conversation of ours. I was still working full-time at this point, so quite a commitment of my precious little free time to make the trip on a weeknight. But Taylor is who I wanted to have a conversation with, because he and I always have incredibly meaningful conversations when we are together hiking, having dinner, or even a phone call. I was always energized after spending time with him, and it felt like our interactions were few and far between, so this was an opportunity for me to create one.

That night in Taylor's condo, after a two-hour convo for the twenty-minute assignment, the seed was planted for what would become The Constant Quest Podcast. We are now in our third year of conversations that have expanded my network of people whom I respect, and I have learned so much more about topics and people than I ever could have imagined. It continues to open new doors and expand my life. Being in school did not mean I had to put everything on hold until I walked across the stage with a degree three years later. The assignment was not a burden. It was an opportunity to create something amazing. Living in concert with my situation.

Does anyone remember a time when the entire world changed overnight, and every routine, social outlet, and plan you had vanished into thin air? The crazy thing about COVID-19 was that it was the same for everyone and different for everyone. Literally the entire world was experiencing its effects at practically the same time. There are several events over my four-plus decades of life where I can remember exactly where I was, who I was with, and what we were doing. I doubt any of those memories will fade any time soon, because they were that impactful. But in all of them—Princess Diana's death, OJ's medium-speed Bronco chase, Columbine, 9/11— there were people throughout the world completely unaffected, uninformed even.

Isn't that interesting? When someone complains about something trivial, a friend of mine responds with, "there are a billion people in India that don't give a shit." A billion! That offers some perspective. No matter the gravity of a situation personally, locally, regionally, or nationally, there are at least millions of people who are oblivious. That is, until COVID. Everyone was in it together.

Our responses, however, varied greatly. Depending on age, regulations, personal decisions, mental health, and life situation, the impact of COVID was also different for each of us. The trajectory of each of our lives changed in some way during the pandemic. Isn't that amazing? One singular event changed us all forever. How did it change you?

Some components we had zero control over: government policy and regulations, how others around us responded, weather and other environmental conditions. Then there were all of the things we could control: physical activity, level of obsession with watching the news, substance use, creativity. How did you change?

There were many negative outcomes during COVID: deaths, job loss, increased domestic violence, substance use, and divorce. I certainly am not here to minimize or discount those who were negatively impacted. There were also many positive outcomes: strengthened relationships, career change, countless creative initiatives brought to life. The latter is a representation of living in concert with your situation.

My state of South Carolina shut down on March 16, 2020. That day, my parents and I were in a waiting room at a local hospital waiting for me to be called back for an inguinal hernia surgery. The staff came out and said each patient could have one person wait for them, so my dad went to wait in the car. After those of us in person in the waiting room were seen, all other elective surgeries were postponed indefinitely.

If there was going to be a time to be forced into little to no activity, I guess the initial lockdown of COVID was about the best. My FOMO didn't flare up too bad, because no one else could do anything either. A few friends teamed up and nursed me back to health in that first week. I was seven and a half months into doing a 5K every single day, and I really didn't want that streak to end. The morning of my surgery, I got up at 3 am just to get a run in before I went under the knife. I asked the surgeon if I could continue my streak the next day. He laughed. He said it would be four to six weeks before being cleared to even jog. I told him I planned to walk it. Unfortunately, the streak came to an interruption for three days. I was frustrated, but haven't missed a day since.

The first ultramarathon I ever ran, the one with Jordan, was in June of 2020. Three months after hernia surgery, and three months into the COVID pandemic. On March 17, 18, and 19, I could not get off of the couch on my own. I first took walks around the house, then outside of the house. Eventually longer walks along rivers and in parks until I was cleared to jog no more than a ten-minute pace for four more weeks. One month after being fully cleared, I ran an ultramarathon.

With the news being informative, and also depressing, I turned to other outlets to spend my time when no businesses were open. When possible I was outside, if not running, then I was on the lake, or in an appropriately distanced yard sitting with friends, which became one of my favorite things to do on a Saturday morning.

My time inside was used to explore creative outlets. I decided with so much time inside, any music I listened to would be an entire album. It was the most fun to consume entire projects of artists, giving me new insight and appreciation. Many of the albums I listened to came as recommendations from friends, tapping into different conversations with people than normal.

In the evenings I practiced my guitar, and taught myself how to edit videos. Such a valuable skill that I have continued to hone and use to this day. It has even been something that people approach me for advice and guidance on. I am not saying I handled COVID better than everyone, and I certainly acknowledge that my situation was extremely fortunate. But it has been inspiring to see and hear stories of how so many people used COVID as an opportunity to positively alter the trajectory of their life forever, living in concert with their situation.

I am interested to know what are some ways that you are living in concert with your situation? We can default by going straight to the areas where we are not living in alignment, or chasing the big thing we have always dreamed of. It might prove helpful to start with some wins. What is going right? What are positive changes you have already made in your life? Can you use that to create momentum and confidence to keep it going? Think of one thing tonight that lights you up. Go through old photo albums, and pay attention to how your body reacts when you see a former version of yourself in particular settings, doing certain activities. If any of them feel inspiring, act on that inspiration! Today is the first day of the rest of your life. Do something that makes you feel *alive*.

REALIZATION

Gratitude

Limitless possibilities

I initially wanted to end the book with this section on gratitude, but it landed here, next to last. As much as I believe presence is a throughline that allows us to enhance the way that we experience life, gratitude has an ever-reaching effect as well. Possibly even a limitless reach. For much of my life, I expected certain things to be there for me simply because they always had been. It took many years to realize that I did not deserve, or had not earned, many of those things. That is not to say I should not use them, but it is to say there are always things in life to be grateful for.

Practicing gratitude helps manage your mood, expectations, and perspective, among many other benefits. You have done all of this work, and it is enough. You are living your life right now, and that is plenty of reason to be grateful. By focusing on positives, you don't ignore the negatives, you simply teach your mind, body, and spirit the peace of appreciation and gratitude. Through all growth, hardship, joy, defeat, and triumph, practice gratitude.

This is not the final credits or anything, but in anticipation of many not reading them, I want to get this off my chest. Thank you. I am grateful for the opportunity to share these pages and words with you, and I am eternally grateful that you have spent this time investing in yourself by reading a book that I authored.

Living in abundance

On five different occasions I have been afforded the opportunity to take a ten-day trip to Bolivia. Travel in general has helped shape my perspective on people, culture, acceptance, and understanding. Travel to places with little to no resources, infrastructure, and stability have really shaped my understanding of joy and gratitude.

My first trip to the country came in 2007, when I was twenty-five years old. As an inexperienced, young professional, I held a skewed view of what it meant to have "a lot" or "a little." My view was that I had very little. A bottom feeder at work, I used every opportunity to show that I belonged by buying things I could not afford. Motorcycle, boat, trips. None of those things ever satisfied, and I constantly needed more. I wore nice clothes, but they weren't the nicest clothes. I had just purchased a house early in 2007, at twenty-five, and all I could think about was making enough money to buy a bigger, better house.

Our internal image of our life completely changes when we realize how much we have. That image we hold affects our mood, our actions, and our relationships. Prior to my experiences in Bolivia, my image had a negative impact. Gratitude changed that.

On that first trip, I had no idea what I had gotten myself into. My brother had been the year prior so I was simply following in his footsteps. Flying into El Alto, just above the capital city of La Paz, was an immediate culture shock. With exhaustion from travel and the altitude, the airport sitting over ten thousand feet, we loaded the bus that was waiting for us outside. As soon as we pulled out of the parking lot, shit got real. There were people everywhere. The buildings appeared to barely be standing. Ahead, a group of people burned tires in the middle of the street. We slowed to navigate the tires, and people were surrounding our bus, hitting the sides, jumping up, and slapping the windows. What in the world have I gotten myself into?

To get to the site where we would work, we had a bus ride that was to take "a few hours." That slowly turned into eight. The first four were like a regular country-road bus trip. Seeing houses, passersby, and paved roads.

Then we turned off of the road and headed into the mountains, where we saw nothing for a few hours. On the most dangerous road I have ever been on, and that is saying something, we eventually encountered a small vehicle with barely any room to pass. It was sleeting, the road was washed out, and the passing vehicle was complete with a live alpaca strapped to the top of it. You cannot make this stuff up.

Finally, we crest a mountain and descend slightly into a village of four homemade buildings. There was no way they knew the rest of the world existed. It's as if we were taking a trip back in time, but it was not back in time. This was a different world than the one I lived in back in South Carolina, but it was the same world.

Any water they drink is scooped and carried up from a river so far down the mountain it is barely visible. Food is harvested on the hillside, and only on very special occasions one of their few animals is slaughtered. The terrain in the Andean altiplano region of Bolivia is extremely difficult to cultivate. It is rocky, high in altitude, and lacking nutrients. Fun fact: Bolivia has more than one thousand different types of potatoes of all shapes, sizes, and colors. It's one of the only things they are able to grow through the winter.

When we pull down into the village and exit the bus, the entire community is gathered in a line singing and dancing to welcome us to their home. It is an emotional experience to see people with so little give so much energy and excitement. There were a couple of drums and Bolivian flutes, which are different length bamboo that you blow over the top of for different tones. The dancing would probably fall into the interpretive category if it were practiced in America, and we all jumped right in.

The people of this village are indigenous Aymaran, and have lived off of this land for generations. We viewed them as having nothing, and to them, they had everything they needed. They were aware that they were poor, by some sense of the word, but not the same way we view it.

Many of them were without shoes, and they slept in shared living quarters on mats on exposed ground, resources severely limited. They had no access to what we consider basic medical care, and no money to exchange for it, or other resources, if they did have access. Their location the opposite of an island, but in the proverbial sense, they very much existed on an island. Disconnected from everything and everyone, but I have never felt more connected to anything in my life.

Gratitude. Everything they truly needed was provided for them. They understand that on a spiritual level, a generational level. Connected to the earth, and connected to one another. All of the "things" that I had back home, that I continuously wanted for, and acquired to reach what I thought was a higher level of satisfaction, suddenly became meaningless.

We were invited to join them one night in some sort of meeting in a building just up the hill. This was the only building with electricity, which ran to the one light bulb in the village on a small wire that looked like a rat had chewed the whole thing. The building was about the size of the little utility shed where I kept my lawn equipment back home, about as big as a detached one-car garage.

After yet another dinner of potatoes and broth, exhausted and sore from digging rock, we walked up the hill to make a quick appearance at their service. We would show face, exchange pleasantries, and head back down the hill for a much needed sleep. Or so I thought.

We opened the door to enter, and the building was slam packed. Already shoulder to shoulder, with every member of the village we were working in, and somehow plus more. I still have no idea where these people came from. There was no room for us, but no one inside seemed to have any awareness, as they all immediately gave us the "come on in" sign.

We filed sideways against the back wall just enough so we could get the door shut and try to spare a few degrees of the near freezing temps. The smell was awful. They did not have the luxury that I had of wiping my body down with WetOnes each morning and evening. I was uncomfortable, tired, and sore, and I considered vomming from the smell. And then the music started.

Music might not even be the appropriate word to use. There were no instruments, just voices. Well, that is not quite accurate either. There was so much more in that room than the voices of those present. There were the voices of all there and all who had ever been there. The pain of those who had gone on, and the hope anointed over those to come. Generations of hardship, challenge, joy, and gratitude.

From the first breath, I completely forgot about the fatigue and smell; they were suddenly nonexistent. Without decision, my body moved up through the crowd of people stopping alongside a few ladies who looked much older than their age. I shared a song book with them, all written in Aymaran. The words were like fifteen characters long, with triple consonants and very few vowels. I made a fair attempt to sing along, which they very much appreciated.

Not being a great singer, I am reluctant to join in, but not here. I sang along like I knew just what I was doing. Like I didn't care who was listening. Eventually drowned out by the piercing, yearning, screaming, imperfectly perfect harmonies of the women with whom I stood.

I closed my eyes. Holding a weathered, calloused hand, swaying back and forth, with tears falling from my eyes. Somewhere in there, as time ceased to exist, I switched from thinking to feeling, from listening to knowing, from wondering to understanding. From pain, sadness, and sympathy to connection, joy, and gratitude. In concert with my situation.

Leaving Marquirivi, Bolivia, was emotionally charged to say the least. My perspective on so many things began to shift, and I felt a transformation happening within me. As we said our goodbyes and went to load up onto the bus, the people of the village offered us a parting gift. They handed each of us a handmade bag, each uniquely its own. Inside the bags were as many potatoes as would fit. They had nothing, and they wanted to give us their possession of highest value, which was the food they grew on the side of the mountain, as a token of appreciation. Gratitude.

Returning to the States after an experience so profoundly meaningful requires a period of adjustment. For me, the adjustment wasn't getting back to the "normal" life I left in South Carolina. Rather, it was learning how to remain the same person I discovered in Bolivia in a place so full of distraction, shiny things, and celebration of personal gain. Boy, I was grateful for everything when we got back. A shower with hot water, a comfortable bed, air conditioning, clean drinking water, reliable transportation, food in abundance.

Being grateful for those types of things was never on my radar before Bolivia. All of a sudden, the "things" I had been chasing lost much of their value and meaning to me. I started to walk outside and recognize how fortunate I am to be able to experience this life and what it offers. It does not mean bad things don't happen, and challenges don't arise, but it does mean that even in those times, we have so much to be grateful for.

When creating the Make It a Month series of monthly goals mentioned earlier, in one of the months I chose to do a month of gratitude. It was a valuable exercise to reconnect with what I felt in Bolivia years before. I highly recommend some form of a gratitude practice be implemented. It might shock you how much you already have on your quest for more.

I wrote down three things each day. First, something that happened in the past day or two. That helped me with presence and managing expectations. It allowed me to reflect on the immediate past and realize something that I received and maybe did not earn.

The second item was a reflection of something from childhood, a larger concept, or spiritual experience. This offered contentment through gratitude, recognizing how fortunate I have been throughout my lifespan.

And the third thing I wrote down each day was a person's name. Relationships ebb and flow, such as life, and I found great value in feeling the impacts people have made on me over the years. It also was a nice exercise in the present allocation of time. The people I feel incredibly grateful for—do I intentionally spend time with them, or at a minimum let them know? So, now I let them know. Right then, because our life is now.

The previous experiences have helped me to create a consistent practice of gratitude. It is a habit that forms, and it has also become a mindset and lifestyle that I try relentlessly to embody. Of course, that ebbs and flows as well, and there are times when gratitude is felt more deeply than others.

One of those such times of deep gratitude was nearing the end of the VanAm trip. I had been to so many states, and cities, and parks. Driven on so many smooth roads and bumpy roads. Mountains, deserts. Gas stations, rest areas. I was so incredibly grateful for every single one of them. It would be months before it all sank in, and I even realized what had just happened, but I felt the magnitude. I was so grateful, because I knew that I did not take a single second for granted. I lived in concert with my situation.

As I was driving back on Interstate 24, south of Nashville, approaching Chattanooga, I remember crossing over Nickajack Lake and breaking out into a wailing sob. I cried my eyes out for several miles, as I crossed the lake and inched farther into the Appalachian Mountains, just down the chain from where my grandparents grew up. The same mountains where Officer Buchanan pulled me over, changing my life forever. I was getting close to the cabins I built in North Georgia on Nana and Pa's land, which is where I was going for a few days. I was so immensely grateful for everything I had experienced, learned, seen, and felt. And only slightly more than that, I was grateful to be home. In everything, gratitude.

REALIZATION

The Time
Is Now

The full send

Thanks to Alanis, we all know the story of the old man who turned ninety-eight, won the lottery, and died the next day. Life is filled with ironies. It is filled with so many things: changes, joys, discomforts, challenges. One thing that does not change in life is that time always wins. You cannot beat time—you simply can't. There is one paradox of time, however, that I have learned from people as they age. It is that time is always the same *and* it speeds up the older you get. If there is any anecdote, or perhaps solace, in that, it is to live your life now. In whatever way you can fully express yourself and take the lead role in your life, the time to do that is right now. No matter your current life situation, your life is now.

"Yes, the best time to have figured it out is before, but the second best time is now, so change it," Naval Ravikant has said. Why do we get in the mindset that, when something did not line up exactly right and blow up at just the right time, we should just scrap the whole thing? My friend Derek calls this phenomenon "sugar or shit." If it is not a ten, we self-sabotage ourselves into a zero. When we do this, we justify it by saving time, avoiding failure, and dodging heartache. But failure is part of success, remember?

I love Naval's quote because it turns perfectionism into permission. Some prior time would have been "perfect," so you don't even have to worry about that anymore. Perfect does not exist today. Your only mission is to do what you can, today, right now. Think about this for a second. What are you actually waiting on?

The ninety-eight year old lottery winner could just as easily have been me or you. A twenty year old, a forty year old. What are we waiting for? The time is now. The cemetery is filled with untapped potential and unrealized dreams. Man, what could I be? Whatever you dream about and visualize is only a possibility if you act now. To save you from flipping or rewinding, I am taking you back to the first page of this book: When are you actually going to do the thing that you are convinced will bring you joy?

In early 2020, I took a trip through Costa Rica and Nicaragua. Near the end of the trip, in Leon, Nicaragua, I caught wind of something called volcano boarding. Being the adrenaline junkie that I am, I had to inquire further. There is a mountain outside of Leon called Cerro Negro, which simply means "black hill." It is black because it's an active volcano. A company, run out of a local hostel, takes people out to ride a board down the side of this active volcano.

They provide the board, and it's quite literally a board. It looks like something my granddad threw together back in the forties to slide down a bank after a snow. It was a flat rectangular piece of wood with two small pieces of wood nailed across short ways. One for your butt and the other for your feet. There was a little string running up through the bottom which doubled as a steering wheel.

The price of the entire excursion, which was to take five hours total, was around $20 USD. You've got to think, even if it is gimmicky, it will be a neat, and quite inexpensive, way to view the countryside and see an active volcano up close.

I learned as I entered the hostel there was a publication in 2014 by CNN that shared "50 of the most thrilling, daring things you can do on vacation." I did a quick Google search to verify that, yes, in fact, volcano boarding in Nicaragua ranked number two on the list. Just one spot behind being a "jet fighter pilot for a day." Um, what? What was number three? What is just less thrilling and daring than what I was about to do on a whim for twenty bucks?

I'll spare you the search. Number three is the cage of death in Australia where you come face to face with saltwater crocodiles for fifteen minutes. And number four is a cliff walk in China where hikers must navigate a slim wooden plank on the edge of a vertical cliff, one kilometer above the ground. Yeah, those were reportedly less adventurous than what I was gearing up to take on.

We had a fifty-minute bus ride to the base of Cerro Negro. Each person with a small cinch bag, housing a body suit and goggles, and their boards. From there a moderate forty-five-ish minute hike up the ridgeline of the volcano, where the only instruction was on how to appropriately hit the deck when the wind gusts were strong enough to throw you off the mountain. Not if, but when.

The entire hike was literally walking over charcoal. At the top, we suited up and prepared for a briefing from our guide. He squatted down, and with his gloves wiped away about two inches of rock. It was smoking. I put my hand about a foot over the area, and it was like holding your hand over an open campfire flame. We really were standing on an eruption waiting to happen.

Ready to get this over with and get the hell out of there, I volunteered to board the mountain first. There were three speeds. Sitting all the way up with the bottoms of your feet skimming the volcanic rock was the slowest speed. Middle speed was to lean back a little with feet still skimming the rock. Top speed was full send: lean all the way back, lift feet, and point them straight out in front of you.

Before turning us loose, our guide felt it appropriate timing to tell us that this is a very consistent, active volcano, never going more than twenty years without erupting in its history. We were having this conversation in February of 2020. I raised my hand and asked, "When was the last time it erupted?" 1999.

Ahh, that is part of the reason this event is on the list of most thrilling and dangerous. I nervously thought about the fact that I could make it off of this ticking time bomb alive and still have a great experience to tell people. But I also thought about our guide, how he would be back tomorrow, next week, next month, and so on. I asked him how he felt about the imminent eruption, and didn't he realize the predicament that put him in?

He smiled calmly and said, "Then I guess I better enjoy today."

Life is now.

And I was off. Full send, leaning so far back my head was nearly touching rock, feet off the ground pointed straight out front. Reaching a top speed of nearly fifty miles per hour, rock flying everywhere, and volcanic smoke in my wake. The time is now.

It wasn't just the act of boarding on the plywood. It wasn't just the fact that we were at a volcano. It was those things, and that it is all fleeting. It can all be gone tomorrow. The next eruption might change the volcano in a way that it can no longer be boarded, my guide might be up there when it erupts. The time is now.

While I was on the road during VanAm, driving back and forth across America, I realized there wasn't much second guessing. When I was at a place, I was there for a period of time and then I was moving on. Although I had no rigid schedule and I could stay somewhere as long as I liked, when I was gone I was gone. So, if a question were to float in my mind whether or not I should do a certain activity that interested me, the answer was always yes. Because there is no other time than now.

Turn in the parking lot, submit a piece of art, share a song; try out for the Atlanta Falcons cheerleading team at forty; change careers, take a van trip across America, start a business; call an old friend, try out for a play, take a walk with your spouse; learn to cook, dance, or play a musical instrument; join a run club, or dance alone in a park just because it feels good.

Engage in *your* life, spend intentional time alone and with others, be present; allow yourself to feel your emotions, be open to change, learn to appreciate impermanence; take it all in stride, step outside of your comfort zone, be grateful for everything; and live in concert with your situation.

The time is now.

Acknowledgments

THIS BOOK IS A product of passion, perseverance, and the generous support of others. I owe a debt of gratitude to the people and places that provided the necessary foundation, both emotional and physical, to bring these pages to life.

To all of the staff and customers of the two extraordinary coffee shops that became my creative playground and writing facility, thank you. You unknowingly fueled this project, one blueberry muffin at a time. A special thanks to Loveland Coffee in Irmo, South Carolina—my order: Blueberry & cream cheese muffin, coffee; and White Birch Provisions in Clayton, Georgia—my order: GF blueberry muffin, peanut butter banana smoothie, coffee. The warmth and genuine conversations had at each of these establishments created the perfect environment for inspiration.

To my mentors, friends, and peers—thank you for being co-pilots on this wild ride of writing, editing, and publishing a book. You encouraged me to keep going, offered guidance when it was most useful, and openly shared your knowledge, expertise, and experience.

More generally, I must thank my incredible community of people who surround me and keep me inspired, motivated, and alive. This includes my family, my childhood friends, my new and old friends, and even the ones I barely talk to. The process of writing this book involved so much reflection; it was therapeutic to revisit the seemingly endless experiences, interactions, and relationships that have helped enrich my life and inform the person I am today.

Finally, to Nikki. You are, quite simply, my rock. The depth of your belief in this book, in several instances, is what kept it going. You didn't just tolerate the emotional roller coaster; you embraced, encouraged, and protected it. When I was lost in the work, you would remind me, with such certainty, that "writing this book is your job right now," and selflessly allowed me to disappear for hours—and sometimes days—to bring my ideas to this work of art. On many occasions, as I would jump out of bed in the middle of the night to scratch out an idea in my iPhone Notes, you just rolled over to grab my hand and said, "get those ideas down, baby!" You were always ready for a reading or a brainstorming session. You see the light in me when I struggle to see it in myself. This book would not exist without your love, strength, and unwavering support. Thank you.

And lastly, I thank me. Nicholas, Nic, and Tine—all of the parts of me.

I thank the current iteration of myself for writing this book, seeing it as both a point of reflection and a dot plotted on my timeline of evolution—a keepsake and a reference point for all future versions of myself.

I am eternally grateful for all prior iterations for taking on challenges and overcoming obstacles; for doing whatever you had to do to build me into the person I am today. For literally staring death in the face, and time and time again, making the decision to KEEP GOING.

Hang in there, buddy, you can do it.

About the Author

NIC COLLINS IS A speaker, life coach, mental health professional, and author dedicated to helping others focus on personal growth, authenticity, and fulfillment.

This book is, in many ways, the book Nic wishes he had read ten years ago—and the one he still needs today. Life experience, education, and years of observation led him to put his realizations on the page after witnessing the widespread epidemic of misalignment, burnout, and lack of fulfillment in our world. Following a transformative two-month van trip across America, he felt an undeniable pull to share the insights gleaned from his personal journey, his background as a mental health professional, and nearly two decades working in corporate America.

With a Master's in Counseling & Rehabilitation, Nic brings both expertise and heart to his message. He vulnerably shares the common challenges and struggles he went through, offering solutions he has found along the way. Above all, he aims to provide a permission slip for the reader: a chance to fully explore themselves and use their unique qualities as the ultimate compass to guide *their* life.

Nic currently lives outside of Columbia, South Carolina, with Nikki; yes, they are Nic and Nikki, how cute. When he isn't speaking or writing, you can find him running a local trail, spending time on the water, or strumming his guitar. His passions of running and live music are reflections of his pursuit of growth and presence, each being equally important, because both can be true. Nic's energy is fueled by deep, meaningful relationships with family and friends, and new inspiring conversations with complete strangers.

To continue the conversation with Nic, you can find him on:
    His website: NicCollinsAuthentic.com
    Instagram: @Nic_Collins_Authentic
    The Constant Quest Podcast, available on all major platforms

Nic Collins
A u t h e n t i c
Speaker. Coach. Adventurer.